Of Some Have Compassion

Being a Good Samaritan to the Mentally Infirmed in a Technological Age.

Mathew Wescott

Cover illustration by Michael Mercadante

All Scripture quotations are taken from the King James Bible, originally translated in 1611.

Published by Of Some Have Compassion llc

ISBN: 979-8-9954585-0-0

Dedication

To my former patients, especially those I picked up from children's hospitals, who broke my heart with their suffering and gave me a burden for people's mental health.

To my friends and family who encouraged me along the way.

And to my Lord and Savior, Jesus Christ, whose loving-kindness and grace enabled a depraved, selfish wretch like me to love others and sustained me through the grueling highs and lows during this process of writing a book that took much more time and effort than I expected. May he receive the glory for any good that comes of it.

Contents

Preface

"Everybody has plans until they get hit." – Mike Tyson (in Raffo, 1987)

Background

The pandemic that began in 2020 hit many and upended what we thought we knew. With regard to mental health, the lockdowns and increased exposures to technology pummeled individuals. On a macro level, our healthcare system was overstretched and may never recover from the demand that event placed on healthcare in general and mental health institutions in particular. There has been an increase in outpatient therapy to try to ease the burden on medical facilities. But it is still too strained. Unfortunately, many churches nearly took a knockout in this area. Most appear unable to correctly recognize and minister to their own, much less reach out into the community and make the impact that God intends for them to have there. At the individual level, during that time working on an ambulance, I encountered many mentally broken people: hurting people who are receptive to kindness, people whom Christ died for, souls who will never realize their potential unless someone has compassion on them.

I have a burden about them because I was around them, and Christianity in general seemed to be doing very little for them. "Why?" I wondered. Could it be that, like the woman of ill repute Jesus met alone at Jacob's well, nobody else wanted to be around them? That does not seem like a wholly plausible explanation, because we have chaplains in jails. Could it be that they could not stand to be around the pain, suffering, and eventual death that often results from mental illness? Once again, with chaplains in hospitals and hospice homes, that did not seem likely. So why were all the mental hospitals that I took patients to chaplain-free?

I had two theories. Maybe people were in denial of this group and their problems. If mental health issues don't exist, we aren't responsible to equip Christians to minister to people with these issues. The second theory was that people who did want to minister to them might have felt inadequate, unprepared, and intimidated because they had so little information about a problem that has become catastrophic in modern times. It is a terrible feeling to know that somebody is hurting, having them open up to you and tell you that they are hurting, and not have the right resources and knowledge to be able to help them. Do that once, and you will rarely ever engage another person on that topic. It feels even worse, however, to share what you were taught on the subject, only to find that your knowledge is disconnected from current reality and confuses and hurts the person you are trying to help. Many times Christians are given poor information about the problem and ways to help, which may be contributing to insecurity and lack of engagement with people suffering from mental health issues.

So I would communicate with my Christian friends to try to raise awareness of these people and to equip others to be compassionate toward them. Several people told me these communications encouraged them and that God would use my unique experiences to be a blessing to others.

Purpose

Many resources are available for mental health. This book is not at all exhaustive. I read thousands of pages in its production, and that is a drop in the bucket compared to the materials available if you would like to research an aspect further.

Some are written by doctors and psychologists, people with all kinds of letters after their names who are much smarter than I am. These people have studied science and seen the order of Creation in the creatures. Many of the ideals and principles they describe are evidenced in the Scriptures. Some of the methods are practical and helpful. Yet inevitably, any work that does not recognize the need for a relationship with a Creator God is incomplete in its conclusions and ends.

Others are written by great spiritual leaders. Some are extreme in that they appear to think every mental problem is a spiritual problem and can be fixed with a biblical solution. But the mind is not spiritual. Some would teach that God miraculously heals all infirmities, including those of the mind, either at salvation or through right faithful living afterward. Although God can miraculously heal minds the same way that he heals bodies, we rarely see either in this era.

A few are more balanced in their approach, recognizing that God instilled order in the universe and gifted humans with wisdom to study science for the betterment of humanity. They will admit that there is a time and place for both spiritual interventions and scientific ones.

This book is written by a nobody with a few years of observations. Its aim is to provide others with a basic understanding of the physical, existential, and spiritual aspects of mental challenges. Through prayer and the help of the Holy Spirit, may it then be used in your life to minister to others.

This book will not give you cookie-cutter solutions or seven-step plans. It will give you information you can take to God to tailor for the individual whom you are trying to minister to. I believe in a doctrine called the "priesthood of all believers," which holds that you can go directly to God for wisdom and many other things. This is a resource to help you build your knowledge and prepare to minister to others.

The point of this book is not to make you agree with it. It is to challenge the stigma and misconceptions around mental health, provide more information to help you reach a balanced conclusion, and then offer practical helps to minister to these people today. From it you may glean something that helps you better minister to others. Many times the conversation is unbalanced and twisted out of context to support an extreme view of the matter. I hope that this book presents enough information to give you a balanced perspective and to clear up some misinformation circulating today. I pray you find it worthwhile.

This book is not designed to be a self-help book. Mental challenges are a hard road to walk alone. This book is designed to better equip you to show mercy on and be a help to others walking this road.

I compiled some of my observations and studies from my time in churches and on ambulances into this book. I have taken a few hundred people to mental institutions over my career and sat under hundreds of religious teachers in my life. This was intended for a wide audience, but not everyone will have the background to understand why I have raised certain issues or made certain points.

Generally, we live in an echo chamber society, where we invite teachers who tell us what we like to hear and silence opposing opinions. Algorithms further isolate us with those who share our beliefs and backgrounds. So if something doesn't sit quite right, consider that someone with a different upbringing or adversity in life may understand exactly what is intended. In my life I have heard hundreds of preachers in dozens of churches across numerous states. Most people think that their perspective, no matter how nuanced, is correct, and many severely overestimate how widely their ideas and definitions are used, even among people with similar religious labels.

I would not go to war with anybody who had a different position outside of the five fundamentals of the faith. I have tried to include things that would be helpful to people from many backgrounds, from those who have lived their whole lives under one wholesome authority system, to those who have had no stability coupled with abusive and competing authorities. Yet those from one background may not understand something included for the benefit of another. You may find some information irrelevant. Others, however, will need it to understand later ideas in the book. If a part does not make sense to you, please use discretion in how you handle it and whether it was intended for you. My hope is that something here can help people from every background that I will never meet in person.

Most people do not like my opinions. The topic of mental health is widely misunderstood by many Christians. It is a generally stigmatized topic. This is a comparatively new field of study in medicine, and it is rapidly changing, as it is influenced by even newer technologies. I make no claims to have the best opinion on the topic. I do not even claim that in a year I will agree with everything that I wrote. The content at some point will likely make you uncomfortable. That is an inevitable result of living in a sin-cursed world. We will not be comfortable around sin while ministering to broken people. This book is simply intended to raise awareness, provide information that may help you while ministering to these people, and provoke you to love and good works. Whether you take what is written and apply it and help people, or you take what is said and help people by trying to prove me wrong and finding a better way, if people are being ministered to in a helpful fashion, glory to God.

Some would argue that everything we need on the topic is found in the Bible and therefore this book is uncalled for. But these people have no problem taking financial classes. They gladly seek out wisdom from those who have done their research. Those who would endeavor to excel in areas such as day trading can learn a great deal from modern financial experts. Although the Bible covers the wise use of money and resources, their studies will include many financial doctrines that people in Bible times could never have dreamed of. Are not people and their mental health more important than finances? Why not use every resource at our disposal to be a good minister in the time into which God has placed us and unto the people whom he has put around us?

Prerequisites

Some things must be established before you are ready to begin. A soldier does not just pick up a gun and go into battle. Much physical and mental training is completed before that soldier is equipped and deployed. This book is likewise intended for those with certain prerequisite competencies.

A Living Relationship With Your Creator

"For as in Adam all die, even so in Christ shall all be made alive" (1 Corinthians 15:22). God our Creator is the source of acceptance, love, hope, and all things good in life. He is perfect in his relationship with us. I cannot describe with words how wonderful it is to be alive in Christ and have a relationship with one who loves and accepts me as his own despite knowing everything about me. He loves me and walks with me in life. Most of us have had earthly relationships that have marred how we view a relationship with a Heavenly Father. But the longer I walk with him, the more I learn of him, the more I want to share him with others and emulate his love to all around me. It is hard to be well if you are still dead. It is equally hard to share the qualities we were created to cherish if you have never properly experienced them yourself.

God gave us the Bible to point us to a relationship with him in Christ. I cannot adequately summarize it in one paragraph, but here is a short overview. Christ died for our sins according to the Scriptures. That is good news, because I know that I am a sinner, but Christ already knows that and has already paid for those sins. The Lord Jesus Christ was buried and rose again on the third day. That is great news, because it shows that just like he had the power to make himself alive again, he has the power to make us alive in him. Acts 16:31 tells us that to apply this good news, we must believe on the Lord Jesus Christ. This is not the same as believing in Santa Claus. There is much evidence that Jesus exists, and when you put your belief on him, your position changes and your whole life changes. This is not simply believing that he exists; if that were the case all the devils would be saved. They all know that he exists. This is a complete trust of who he is and acceptance of what he will do. As Lord, he is the Creator and authority for all of his creation, and you acknowledge and accept that. As Jesus, he is God who became a man and lived a sinless life to die in your place and take the penalty for your sins so he could be your Savior. As Christ, he is the coming ruler who will judge sin and sinners and set things right in his kingdom. For more information about this read the Bible. I recommend starting in the book of Romans.

A Proper Understanding and Use of Love as a Motivator

The previous verse to our theme concept states, "Keep yourselves in the love of God, looking for the mercy of our Lord Jesus Christ unto eternal life" (Jude 1:21). If you are not in the love of God, you cannot completely understand compassion.

There are many places in the world where we might look for love. There is a love that should exist as a parent for their child. There is a love among siblings and friends. There is a love from romance that eventually should bring the strongest form of commitment, self-control, and self-sacrifice possible from a human.

The problem with each of these expressions of love is that they are corrupted. If they exist in a person's life (and I do understand that some people have never experienced any form of love), they are imperfect at best. They are limited, may be self-serving, or have any number of imperfections. These imperfect manifestations of love become our idea of what love is. They set the bar for how we can express that love to others.

What is the gospel?

Mark 1:1
The beginning of the gospel of Jesus Christ, the Son of God;

Mark then proceeds to write a whole book about the gospel of Jesus Christ - often shortened to "the gospel." But make no mistake, all of the good news in the world is because of him. He came and was born of God through a virgin, with the sinless blood of God flowing through his veins. He lived a sinless life. He was sentenced to death for the crime of being a King who wasn't the Roman Caesar. He was crucified and shed his blood. He died. But after being in the ground for three days and three nights, he rose again proving his power over death and hell! Through this he paid for our sins. He did not need to experience one bit of the suffering he endured because he was the sinless Son of God. He chose to for us.

That's all cool, but the best part is that he can now offer us his eternal life and his relationship with God the Father because he paid our debt with his sacrifice. His offer is so simple and generous it is hard to believe. He offers us a home in Heaven, acceptance into the family of God, and so many more good things if we will just turn from our ways and accept his payment for our sins through faith in his name.

Romans 5:17 For if by one man’s offence death reigned by one; much more they which receive abundance of grace and of the gift of righteousness shall reign in life by one, Jesus Christ.

These are the core elements of the gospel.

But our relationship with God gives us a perfect model of his love. As the relationship grows, our understanding of what love should be becomes more correct, and it increases our motivation to share something so wonderful and so necessary with others.

Be Sufficiently Healed to be Able to Help Others

Someone who has just been beaten and is lying down by the road cannot well help another injured man. You may need some healing before you can help others. Localized injuries may reduce your effectiveness and abilities. I cannot work on the ambulance well with a broken femur. If there were no other option, I would give it a shot.

In the same manner, sometimes problems with insecurity, pride, relationships, anger, bitterness, or other things may reduce your effectiveness in this ministry. Some of these problems may be contagious. Others may cause more injuries to those who need assistance. If, for example, I have an injured ankle and it breaks while I am trying to lift you, I am likely to drop you and cause more injury. Although it would not necessarily stop me from trying to help if I saw someone beside the road dying, it would be risky and limiting. Sometimes there are no better options, and we must take the chance, possibly hurting others in the process. But it is far preferable to be healed and fit before making the attempt, if possible.

If you have challenges in this area, many other authors have taken the Bible and compiled Scriptures and principles to address common difficulties. Seek out spiritual ministers in a local church that preaches the whole Word of God, both pleasant and difficult. They are often the best option for helping individuals with their challenges, using the Scriptures and, at times, good books. Once you have received help and healing, you will be better ready to use this book to minister to others.

Disclaimer

"The older I get, the more I learn. The more I learn, the less I know." – Unknown

I am a human. There will be errors in this book. Some of this information will be dated by the time it is published. Other information will likely be proven wrong in the coming years.

You will probably disagree with opinions, emphasis, tone, and even information in this book. I apologize in advance. I have done my best, through prayer and study, to write something that will be a help to others. But the truth at times offends people, and I am a flawed human trying to present truth. Please do not allow an imperfect presentation to cloud your opinion toward the truths herein.

I am not God or a doctor. This information is not a substitute for medical or spiritual advice. You assume all responsibility for how you use the information in this book and any associated consequences.

This book and most of the books referenced herein are intended for a mature audience.

I have referenced many good books on the topic throughout this work. That does not mean that I endorse or agree with everything they say. By their nature as medical books and the subject matter they deal with, there will be things in them that some think should not be discussed or printed publicly. I'm glad they are. I think that every book I referenced is worth reading. The issues exist. I want to know as much as I can about them so I can be as well-equipped as possible to help those who are struggling. Other individuals have different tolerances. User discretion is advised.

Chapter 1: The Good Samaritan: Compassion and Love

"Thou shalt love ... thy neighbour as thyself." – Luke 10:27

"But he, willing to justify himself, said unto Jesus, And who is my neighbour?" (Luke 10:29). Jesus proceeded to answer this lawyer's question with a parable. In this parable we have two law-keepers who failed to attend to the injured man's needs and might even have used the law to justify their inaction. The protagonist in this parable is a Samaritan, one who did not even know what to worship or where to worship. Yet Christ said to learn from him how to love people. So if we are to do likewise, we should consider what this love involved and whom the recipient was.

The Neighbor

This recipient could be anyone. We are not told a thing about his heritage or his background. He could have been nobility, or he could have been disabled. Age, skin color, religion, and net worth are never mentioned about this man. All we know is that one day some sinners got to him. They left him exposed and vulnerable, injured and dying. At this point, nobody could tell anything about him. Any clothes or possessions that might have indicated his social status were all taken away.

In his condition, he was unaware of his state. The Bible uses the term "half dead." I do not know what that meant when it was translated, but on the ambulance today we use an AVPU(d) scale to measure from alert to dead. Halfway is the "P" for pain. At that rating, he would not have seen anybody walking by. He would have never known that the priest and the Levite were there. (I'm sure others put the pieces together after the fact. They likely realized that the priest and Levite just walked right past the injured man and had done nothing. Then religion just became even less attractive to them.) The only thing that he knew in that state was pain. The only things he would have noticed were those which increased or relieved that pain. You could have walked up to him and yelled his name, but it would not have registered. You could have told him that he was dying, and he would not have heard or cared. This is the mental state of many today, injured and half dead, completely oblivious to their state, not even noticing people around them who could possibly offer assistance, and not strong enough to muster a cry for help. He needed somebody to notice him. He needed somebody to recognize his state. He needed someone to show mercy on him. Left on his own, he would die.

The Love

The Samaritan was not a perfect human. As was already mentioned, he was confused in his worship. He had a terrible heritage and was despised by the people of that area for it. Yet he had a natural love for his neighbor untainted by concerns of the law. The pure love he showed to this dying man was second only to the love Christ showed to us. When we really look into it, there are many details about just how intense this love was and how ours should be on those around us.

He Loved More Than He Was Repulsed

We read this parable on clean black-and-white paper in a sheltered, sanitary environment. It is easy to forget that he was walking up to a naked, limp, battered, and bloody man lying in the dirt and mud on a dangerous highway! Flies could have been swarming around, laying eggs on blood and flesh. He could have been missing an eye or two. You might have been able to see his intestines or his brain. (No, I am not making this up. I have seen people like this who survived!) No matter what condition a person is in, how long they have been in that condition, or how repulsive they and their situations may seem to us, we must love them anyway.

He Loved Despite Significant Risks to His Social Status

There was a risk of being misunderstood, maligned, and falsely condemned. There was a risk of his time and resources being "wasted." In his day with the stereotypes, if the man died under his care, he was even at risk of being executed!

He Loved Regardless of the Financial Cost

He used his personal wine and oil. He bound him with his own bandages. He left an open tab with the innkeeper after paying 2 days' wages up front for the man's care. We do not know how much this man's care ended up costing the Samaritan, because the point of the parable is that it was without limit.

He Loved Without Getting Thanked

In fact, for all we know, after he was healed the injured man might have complained about the Samaritan and the level of care he received or about the permanent injuries he suffered. He could have blamed them on the one trying to help instead of on their real source. He could have just been an entitled ingrate. He might have cursed the fact that it was a Samaritan who helped him and claimed that he would rather have died!

He Loved Without Knowing if it Made a Difference for the Injured Man

For all the Samaritan knew, he was just delaying an inevitable death. The man might never have fully recovered and just cost everybody extra time and expense until he died days or months later.

He Loved Despite the Danger to His Personal Safety

We already mentioned the dangers of being misunderstood in an ethnically charged environment. The robbers who got the man might not have been far away, or they might have decided to come back looking for more. Other robbers might have been in the area. The danger of animals coming to the scent of blood was real, as lions and bears lived in those mountains at the time.

He Loved Despite the Inconvenience and Extra Effort Required

With the injured man riding on his beast, now he had to walk the rest of the way to the inn. Whatever plans he might have had would be delayed. People who were expecting him might have been concerned for his well-being or disappointed if he missed a connection.

This was the level of love from the man (who belonged to a group Jesus called out for being totally confused in their worship) whom Jesus chose to use to model our mercy and compassion as neighbors. This love became a focal point of the early church.

Chapter 2: Technology's Influence and the Decline of Mental Health

"TELEPHONE, n. An invention of the devil which abrogates some of the advantages of making a disagreeable person keep his distance." – Ambrose Bierce (1911)

Mental Health Challenges Are Increasing at an Alarming Rate

Mental health challenges have always existed, but they seem more pervasive now than ever before. Some would blame this increase on better awareness, but I do not believe that tells the whole story. Certain factors that contribute to mental and cognitive decline are now much more prevalent. I believe that technology is a major adverse factor in this arena.

How has technology affected our mental health, and why is it relevant? Large quantities and types of technology have been engineered to make them more addictive and less healthy mentally and physically, from foods to medicines. I will limit the scope of this book to technology that employs programming and frequencies. Much attention currently is being given to the potentially addictive and depressing nature of social media. As long as there has been money to be made off a product, it has been engineered to make it as appealing/addicting as possible while hiding its known destructive effects. Most technologies and their uses have these characteristics today.

There appears to be a profound lack of awareness and understanding that the problem has changed with the world around us. These changes are accelerating rapidly as our technology becomes more pervasive. It is more prevalent and harder to deal with now than ever before.

It annoys and frustrates me today to hear people referring to younger generations as weak, often with derogatory slurs and nicknames. I wish I could tell every one of them, "Just imagine if you had to deal with all this busyness and stress that you have today while you were a teenager in high school. Do you think you might be overwhelmed and facing significant challenges?" People today are doing just that. They are running from classes to events to team activities, trying to maintain a social life, and trying to figure out how they will survive. They are trying to find their place in an increasingly expensive, hostile, and frightening world while burning the candle at both ends. They are dealing with record family turmoil (as evidenced by divorce rates, children born to unwed parents, and abuse and neglect statistics), consuming caffeine and other chemicals being marketed as food and drinks (that are just trying to get you hooked so you spend more on them), and much more. They are doing all of this while their brains and bodies are still forming. Many are doing it all without being aware of all of the disadvantages modern technology has placed upon their mental health. It affects older people too, but it seems to affect those without the awareness and discretion that come with maturity at a much higher rate.

Many of These Negative Effects Have Been Caused by or Exacerbated by Modern Technology

Technology has increased speed, awareness, busyness, complexity, and stress in this generation. Presences are maintained across a variety of platforms, and each demands attention and acceptance. Nearly all of them also come with stressors.

Behavioral Changes

One of the areas in which technology has changed our lives is our behavior. Our habits as we go about our day are markedly different from those of 200 years ago. It seems obvious that most of these lifestyle changes have come with significant disadvantages.

Possibly the most wide-reaching of those disadvantages is sleep deprivation. Two hundred years ago, we were dawn-to-dark people. The only exceptions would have been with the use of candles, oil lamps, and campfires. One hundred years ago, electricity was becoming common. Where it was available, we could now work around the clock, conveniently extending our workday at the expense of sleep as needed. Now we take screens with backlights to bed with us! The blue light in these screens has been shown to keep our brains awake and unable to repair even when our bodies are tired, just like many other stimulants. If we are studying or viewing intense materials, more of our brain is involved and not down for repair. It is ever easier to reduce our available time for sleep by using it on our phones or televisions.

Besides reducing our brain's ability to function, lack of sleep causes stress and chemical imbalances. The hormones leptin and ghrelin, both affected by sleep deprivation, affect the metabolism. If technology contributes to insufficient sleep, insufficient sleep contributes to obesity, and obesity contributes to all kinds of health and quality-of-life problems, then technology is causing us a problem. These are just two of the many hormones sleep deprivation affects. The stress and lack of repair from sleep deprivation cause both psychological and physical impairment. None of this is good, but this is only the beginning.

Technology keeps us too busy. We no longer need to stand over the pot and stir it while our minds rest. Program the microwave for 60 seconds and spend 58 of them scrolling through Facebook while you wait. The person who introduced me to this idea, Dr. Holly Haynes with Truett McConnell University, spoke of the waiting involved in the creation of mix tapes. I am a millennial. I had never even heard of mix tapes before. (You can use technology to try to get an understanding of how they were created and the waiting involved.) Playlists made them obsolete and eliminated yet another opportunity for a breather among the bustle of life. We need times to be still. Think with me for a bit. How much awake time do you spend in a day without external stimuli?

In contrast, technology also keeps people too inactive. Now we have so many "desk jobs" in our world. We know that exercise is good for the body. We also have recognized that it is good for the mind. It increases our happiness. It improves our memory function.

We recognize that adults need to be active, especially if they work at a job where they sit all day. But what does inactivity do for kids? Kids were created naturally to be active. Now they spend all their free time sitting in front of a screen because they enjoy it. Then we wonder why they can't sit still in a classroom that they do not enjoy. Technology may be helping our kids become hyperactive when they are not being stimulated by a screen. Inactivity also may be contributing to other health problems such as obesity, which in turn causes mental problems. Technology has replaced activity and increased the physical and mental health problems we experience.

Children do not play as much anymore. Little brains are not exercised as frequently, which they need to develop. Children do not get bored enough to need to learn how to entertain themselves. Their imaginations do not need to be as vivid. They are constantly being stimulated by lights, movement, sounds, and screens. When they are being entertained, their problem-solving skills are not being developed. They are not learning how to handle disappointments or how to wait patiently for help. The level of physical activity and interpersonal interaction is reduced. I'm not saying screen time needs to be completely banned, though that might not be a bad idea. But it should be given sparingly, like a dessert after a meal. These reduced in-the-moment physical interactions and development seem to be setting them up for mental deficiencies later in life.

Social Interactions

Technology has changed not only our lifestyles and behaviors, but also our social interactions. Socializing can be stressful. Socializing in a wicked society is even more stressful. Socializing in multiple environments all at the same time, some real but most virtual, seems to amplify that stress exponentially, especially for those who have a hard time separating the virtual from reality. These changes to our social interactions are almost universally more negative than positive.

Technology has replaced in-person friendships. We need our friends. God designed us as social creatures. Sociologists have posited that we need three to four really close friends to help us in life, and that keeps us from desperately trying to befriend everyone we encounter to that level and from being frustrated when it doesn't work. Besides that, we need friends who come and go through various phases of our lives. These are good, necessary things. Yet we do not spend enough time talking to each other anymore to have friends. Social activities are virtually obsolete. If we get together, we do not talk; we watch a movie or play video games. That makes for a good time, but communication is the foundation for relationships. We all know that our friends on social media aren't real. Deep down, we know that we're not real on there, either. People we connect with online do not really know us, and we only know whatever act they want to post. Many are literally starving for friendship due to technology, even though people are all around them.

Along that same vein is the increased isolation. We do not have barn raisings anymore. We do not go to Friday night community events. COVID-19 killed whatever was left of them. We hardly even hang out at the park. Now we're in a basement playing video games. We are in a Discord chat room with our "friends" who will not be there for us in a real need because they have never met us in real life. We are streaming on Twitch or Netflix. We work from home, study from home, shop from home, and party at home. If we do go out, we keep personal contact at a minimum by paying for our gas at the pump, using self-checkouts, and such. If we get in trouble or have a question, there is no need to have personal connections or to know whom to ask. Google is to the rescue! For that matter, older people and their knowledge are almost irrelevant. We do not need to spend time sitting and listening to them ramble anymore while we are trying to get on with our busy lives. We can now live as hermits in the middle of the city!

As comical as it is to follow up this way, we are also too intertwined through technology. Everybody's problems in our social media feed become our problems. We must fight multiple battles simultaneously. There is a compelling need for interactions with our posts. If the numbers of likes and followers start going down, it is time to panic. We even monitor whether or not our messages get read! We are members of a dozen different group chats and apps. We can't even keep up with all of our connections, and it is stressing us out. Then, if we do not respond (or get a response) in a timely fashion, those potential or missed connections become a source of stress as well!

Technology has made being a busybody much, much easier. It used to be that someone had to go from house to house to spread tall tales. Then with the telephone they could simply sit around and gossip as much as they could afford. Now we have our choice of where and how to spread it. Do you want a chat room? How about social media? Maybe just a direct message will do. Or how about a disappearing direct message?

All of these connections mean fewer opportunities to heal. Did you do something embarrassing? Cameras are everywhere now. It is going to end up on the internet and go viral. In the past, you could have moved on by the time you woke up the next morning. Your friends would have forgotten about it in a week. Now, they can watch and rewatch every detail. That video will be trending for months. And instead of being a fuzzy, in-the-moment memory, it will be emblazoned in high definition on your friends' memories for the rest of their lives. They can also pull up and show you so that you can remember all of the details. (On the bright side, the vast quantity of footage that is out there means that less focus can be given to any one event. However, online bullying exists, and the situation is definitely worse than not having cameras at all.) Did you break up with someone? Every time you log into social media, someone will be talking about them. You will see their pictures all over the internet. Did you say something? Expect it to be blown out of proportion, taken out of context, and debated across all public forums. Then expect to be maligned for months, not given the chance to defend yourself, ostracized or nearly executed, often by people whom you thought were friends. You do not even have time to process one assault and move on before the next one comes. Technology has made crises last so long that we literally go from one crisis to the next, with no time to heal in between.

In a similar vein, privacy has been significantly compromised. Both unwelcome invasions of privacy and voluntarily sharing too much have similar results. The unwelcome intrusions, whether hacking, espionage, or another form, feel most violating. This is especially true when it involves discovering or sharing things that are demeaning or embarrassing. Yet even voluntarily giving up privacy leaves you more susceptible to others' opinions and their related pressures. You may find yourself in lower esteem for letting others into an area that you thought was perfectly normal and acceptable.

To make matters worse, now we can create deepfakes that will fool most people into believing that you really are some kind of buffoon or villain. A more publicized problem as of late is that artificial intelligence (AI) can draw in minutes what it took a skilled person hours with a quality program to do a decade ago. The results may be humorous when people use AI to create deepfakes of the Simpsons predicting calamities after the event has happened. They are quite stressful when people use them to create images and videos that are distributed on the World Wide Web to destroy a person's reputation. We cannot keep up with the creation and distribution of these. Even Taylor Swift, with all her resources and followers, cannot get ahead of them. My hope is that as these types of degrading and demoralizing pictures and videos become more common, their impact on individuals will be lessened because a community that recognizes they are just frauds will come to the affected people's aid. Cultivating a group of close-knit friends who know you is becoming a necessity, because soon there will be enough mistakes and misinformation online to destroy all of our public esteem. If you can get a few friends who know you and will stick by you, do not worry about the rest.

These fakes and posed photos also create an artificial idea of normal. We begin to think of facades as reality. We begin comparing our lives to a staged social media presentation and feel totally deficient. The artificial relationships, unnatural displays of affection or status, and overall totally happy, healthy presentations tend to create discontent with our own circumstances, abilities, and relationships. This weighs on our esteem and causes stress. Before the internet, you actually had to go somewhere to deal with actors. Now you can see them every day, all day, from the comfort of your home!

Thought Life

It is obvious that thoughts can have a direct effect on mental health. Most of the thoughts that technology is introducing are not good ones. That will likely affect us negatively in the long run.

Technology has increased our knowledge. We have a world of information and propaganda at our fingertips. We now have kids in grade school worried about whether they might have been born in the wrong body. People in high school are afraid that the world is coming to an end. Why? It is because issues that would otherwise be a problem at the local level have gained national attention through our media. I believe the climate has been deteriorating for 4,400 years. We are just aware of it now because of our technology. The propaganda sets the tone for the discussion. If the people online are panicking or ready to go to war over a (non)issue, the people reading it are conditioned to do the same. We weren't designed to have the knowledge of evil at all. Now we are bombarded with it constantly. I know a teenage girl who was struggling with anxiety. She told me one of the triggers the previous week was that in her town a father had been arrested for abusing his daughter. She found out about it the night of the arrest through her phone. News like that has the biggest impact when it is fresh, and the impact of almost any news that makes the internet is not usually positive. You can watch the news today and in 1 hour see more evil from around the country than people 100 years ago saw in their community for a whole week! At all levels, knowledge is increasing due to technology, and the type of knowledge we are exposed to is vexing our souls and harming our minds and bodies.

Technology keeps us distracted from what is actually important. It competes with sleep, friendships, productivity, relationships, worship, and a host of other things. Yet when it keeps us from fellowship with our Creator God, it opens the door for all kinds of challenges. Social media begins to have more influence than the very Word of God because it is consulted first and more than the Bible. If we are not careful, it can steal time from the Scripture reading and prayer and become an idol. This causes spiritual stress, which affects other parts of the human.

If you are struggling with trauma, technological triggers abound! If clowns conjure up bad memories, has technology got clowns for you! Look out for them on social media, in the news, and expect them to even make an occasional appearance in your TikTok reels. The same goes for violence and broken homes. If you have lost somebody you love, there are plenty of opportunities to reopen that wound. If war zones do it for you, we can put a new one in the news every day. If talk of suicide puts unpleasant thoughts in your head, you can find it on the set and on the net. These are just some of the major triggers people deal with. They do not affect everybody the same, which is why they can be mainstream while still tragically harming some. The faster we absorb knowledge while scrolling, the faster we receive its negative effects, and the more likely we are to find things that trigger negative effects on our psyche. Technology has increased the rate at which we encounter them.

There also has been an increase in the availability of poisons for the mind. I can't tell you how many people I have met through the years who were being poisoned from a young age by the television (and now the internet). They were absorbing garbage at a rapid clip, unaware of its potential destruction, until they experienced major trauma. That proved to be the catalyst that activated years' worth of poisons that had been stored in the mind in high-definition memories. Now the person is dealing with not only the trauma, but also the weight of all the memories that now have a new meaning and new power. Even when they are not directly thinking about the event, related scenes from this video clip or that movie come to mind and are almost as oppressive.

I'll give you a personal example that is relatively minor compared to what some people suffer, just to help you understand this concept. Growing up, I watched a lot of westerns. In many of them, a man with a family is murdered. The movies make those scenes seem so light, and ordinary people get their sense of reality from what they see on television. Well, on the ambulance we got a call out to try to save a man who had been shot in the head in front of his girlfriend with their kids in another room. He was beyond saving. The hysteria of the girlfriend and the shock of the children cannot be depicted by any skill of acting. But now all of those Western movies have a new reality. I understand they are just actors, but they are depicting events that actually happened. Other genres depict things that could happen. So now, if I were to watch a western (and I do not because it bothers me too much), when that head of the household dies, I wouldn't see the actors' muted reactions on screen. I see the shock and hysteria of reality, and know that it happened time and again to real people. That is just from being a third party to a traumatic event. I can't help but wonder what poisons such as *The Parent Trap* (Meyers, 1998) feel like to children whose parents are going through a divorce or how depictions of violence feel to people who have experienced it.

There is so much shown on technology that we do not register as poison because we haven't experienced the catalyst. The more I live, the more I am convinced that we are doing irreparable damage to children's minds not only by what we let them watch, but also by what we watch in their presence. I am shocked as an adult by watching so many things I saw in my childhood and realizing that there were dark things in kids' shows. Some of them my parents probably didn't even recognize because they weren't exposed to that part of the world in their lives. Even cartoons are full of adult innuendos that I never picked up on. As an adult watching the same cartoons I'm thinking, "Wow! I can't believe they put that in a kid's show." Between the internet and interacting with baser elements in society, I've come to understand the damage many of the productions by the Devil's minions are doing to developing minds. It is planting mines that are often triggered in junior high and high school settings.

Then, there are other poisons that people of a certain maturity or life experience know immediately are having an ill effect on them. I already mentioned that I do not watch westerns anymore. Seeing the wickedness of violence and murders has an immediate ill effect on me. In fact, I have a hard time watching most things on television or the internet. I have seen the real-life results of so much sin that most films trigger far worse images in my mind. (I do not want to ever "get over it," although I probably could. I fear that would sear my conscience and reduce my compassion and ability to help others who are in those situations, hurting and needing help in real life.) Then there is much potential for things that we all know are universally harmful and immediately destructive to everyone online. We have easy access to the poisons of anger, strife, and debate. Technology fuels the poisons of jealousy and covetousness. You know immediately that you are worse off than before when these poisons start having their effects.

Pornography is one such poison. I believe that because of too much focus on it and sex in general, the hype adds to the problem. One issue is that the excessive focus distracts us from other issues that enter our lives and begin to poison and weaken us. Pornography is not more harmful than any other addiction or idolatry, but it has become a focal point for a battle. We are subsequently more susceptible to concurrent destroyers. Also, we keep putting it in front of people to the point that those who would not think much of it and simply pass when the opportunity arises cannot get away from thinking about it. We actually add to the problem we are trying to prevent by keeping it in front of people's faces and minds, providing details about how accessible it is, and discussing how dangerous and appealing it is. Some have turned victory over pornography into an idol in its own right. But pornography is bad, and the internet has made it worse in our culture.

Lies introduce poison very subtly. It is like our rat or ant bait. There is a lot to like about it, but the poison is time-released. Children are told, "If you believe, anything is possible." (Christians take Scripture, like Philippians 4:13, out of context to teach the same thing.) Eventually they realize that there are no magic shoes. There are real limitations physically, intellectually, and socioeconomically. That reality eventually hits them like a ton of bricks because they have been weakened by lies since they were old enough to watch the television. Older children are told, "Follow your heart." They end up bankrupt, with a cheapened and broken body, and feeling worthless and hopeless because they gave everything they had to follow their heart, only for their heart to lead them astray and hang them out to dry.

Some lies are more implied than spoken. Gone are the days of *Old Yeller* (R. Stevenson, 1957), where stories introduce irreversible tragedy, and you are shown how to accept it and move on. Now every story has a perfect ending in which all the protagonists are alive and happy. Then when something bad and final happens in real life—you get the idea. In a similar vein, children are programmed to believe that every wrong can be made right and that its effects can be reversed. In life, actions have consequences that usually can't be reversed for the victim. There also may be consequences that society imposes for infractions of a certain magnitude. Some people's first realization of this comes after they have done something serious to a person they care about and they can't make it right, or after law enforcement puts them in handcuffs. They believed lies that did not prepare them for reality, and this made the lies that much more difficult to handle when reality finally showed up.

The last and worst poison I will mention with technology is one of the first and most subtle: pride. Technology is all about how we feel and self-gratification. We want to be noticed. We want to be liked. We want to feel connected. We want to be aware of the problems of the day. We want to watch programming that makes us feel good. We want to win the game. We want our position to be right AND get majority support. (Good luck with that one!) We want to remove or block anything that challenges us or brings us pain. Now we even have individual devices for everyone in the house so we can all be gratified to the fullest at the same time! Then when life actually hits us, and it is not all about us, and we can't do whatever we want, the poison has made us weaker to deal with real life. Pride has a harder-to-see effect on our mental health, but it is possibly the worst destroyer.

I hope this has allowed you to see more clearly the terrible side effects of modern technology on people's minds. Maybe it will enable you to show more compassion to those afflicted by it, especially those who were exposed to it in their formative years, addicted to it by their teens, and now with an insufferable amount of poison filling their minds, just waiting for a catalyst to set some of it off. They are facing huge disadvantages, particularly in their mental state, that people in previous generations cannot begin to understand. So how do you help the people dealing with these effects?

Chapter 3: Misconceptions That Influence What We Believe About Love and Mental Health

"He who controls the message controls the masses."
– attributed to Paul Joseph Goebbels (as cited in everything2, 2003)

Before we lay a foundation to help people, we must clear up some misconceptions. These may prevent us from accurately receiving the truths in the next chapters. We want a clear, level mind on which to build this foundation.

There is much confusion and cross-application of terminology to the point where one finds himself ripe for criticism any time he dares to speak on the subject of mental health in a "Christian" setting. I am going to attempt to clarify and avoid as much confusion as possible when I am writing about the topic. There are two main areas from which confusion originates: definitions and beliefs.

In his parable, Jesus expertly challenged the lawyer's assumptions and preconceived notions on multiple fronts with relatively few words. His overarching theme was challenging the lawyer's narrow definition of his neighbor as it related to his obligation to love. But in the process he challenged the beliefs of the law as it applied to the religious leaders of his day.

I am not trying to challenge or control anybody or anything. I am simply trying to present reasoned information to help you make an informed decision by pointing out some pitfalls that have been introduced into discussions on this topic. My goal is to be verbose enough that there is no misunderstanding. You may agree or disagree, but I want to be clear. That will take a little bit longer than Jesus did. However, I do not want to be so wordy that it becomes tedious. I hope to strike a balance that leaves you understanding where the confusion is, the reasons for the various positions, and which ones I believe are current or correct.

Definitions

When it comes to definitions, there are two main reasons confusion may arise. We will look at each in more detail.

Definitions Change Over Time

The first reason is completely normal and appropriate. In every language, the definitions of words change over time. Some words do not have the same meaning today that they did hundreds of years ago. Even the word *psychology* has changed from its original etymological definition, "psycho" (soul) and "logia" (study). Although biology still studies life and geology still studies the earth, psychology no longer studies souls. While this is normal and accepted, problems arise when people do not respect the changing definitions in society and continue to use antiquated definitions in modern conversations. A very prominent example as it pertains to our interests in this subject is the lightning-rod word *mind.*

Consider this definition in Bailey's (1721) dictionary: "The reason or rational part of the soul." Now let's look at the modern definition from the *New Oxford American Dictionary* (A. R. Stevenson & Lindberg, 2010): "The element of a person that enables them to be aware of the world and their experiences, to think, and to feel; the faculty of consciousness and thought. ... A person's mental processes contrasted with physical action."

For reference, I have also included a description of the word *mind* from Sir Walter Raleigh as preserved in Johnson's (1755) *A Dictionary of the English Language*:

> This word being often used for the soul giving life, is attributed abusively to madmen, when we say that they are of a distracted mind, instead of a broken understanding: which word, mind, we use also for opinion; as, I am of this or that mind: and sometimes for men's conditions or virtues; as, he is of an honest mind, or a man of a just mind: sometimes for affection; as, I do this for my mind's sake: sometimes for the knowledge of principles, which we have without discourse: oftentimes for spirits, angels, and intelligences: but as it is used in the proper signification, including both the understanding agent and passible, it is described to be a pure, simple, substantial act, not depending upon matter, but having relation to that which is intelligible, as to his first object: or *more at large thus; a part or particle of the soul, whereby it doth understand, not depending upon matter, nor needing any organ, free from passion coming from without, and apt to be dissevered as eternal from that which is mortal.* (Emphasis mine)

The older word/definition is completely connected to the soul. It conveys a sense of power even greater than our modern *will*. Sir Raleigh was executed by King James I and would have had keen insight into the meaning of words during the time of the Bible's 1611 translation.

By contrast, the modern mind is connected to the physiological. It is not directing but experiencing. These two words could not be more different after 400 years, yet they are the same word.

Many who want to talk about the mind from a biblically authoritative standpoint have never actually studied it beyond confirming their preconceived notions. As such, most have no idea that the Biblical mind is different from the modern medical mind. In the Bible, the mind is definitely a volitional thing. It can be willfully changed. It can be renewed. It can be spiritual, carnal, double, and so on. It is always closely associated with the will and the soul. By contrast, in modern terminology and medicine it refers to the thinking/feeling experiences of the body, especially the brain, and by extension the hormones and other molecules that affect it. This difference is critical. When people try to take Scriptures that reference things such as "renewing your mind" (which in its Scriptural context of the biblical definition for mind can be done) and try to apply it to physiological mind conditions such as posttraumatic stress disorder or chronic traumatic encephalopathy (which cannot be renewed until the glorified body is received in the rapture), we cause frustration.

It is often said that frustration directed inwards turns to depression and directed outwards turns to anger. Scripture taken out of context, if it is sincerely believed and attempted, can be a catalyst for depression and anger. Until you have studied the issue thoroughly with guidance from the Holy Ghost, please do not parrot trite cliches and religious-sounding solutions. It is confusing and dangerous to take a biblical term and a medical term and mix up their contexts and applications.

Definitions Can Be Fabricated for Control

The second reason definitions cause confusion is less acceptable. There are people, often leaders of cult-like groups, who make up their own definitions of words. This allows them to present as if they have knowledge that the general populace doesn't. Often, when these people are challenged on their positions and definitions, they resort to other unacceptable tactics (intimidation, gaslighting, and so on) to maintain the belief that they are right. Others under their influence adopt their definitions. Eventually you end up with groups of people who believe, teach, and act upon cult-made definitions. Some know their definition is erroneous (they may follow willingly or begrudgingly), while others genuinely believe it is true because they trusted their teachers. Either way, it creates a large disconnect between the group and its teachings and the world around it that we must minister to.

As an example of this, I recently heard a man teach about depression. He used Elijah as an example. He outlined all of the steps Elijah took to eventually overcome it. The people who attended the meeting left happy. The man had stated what they wanted to hear: that depression was treatable with a biblical prescription. They were encouraged. The only problem with the whole situation was that Elijah never had depression. I'm not sure exactly where the speaker got that idea. It seemed to be from the fact that Elijah wanted to die. (I will discuss Elijah and this aspect of his life in further detail in the soul chapter.) But over 1 in 5 American high school students admitted to contemplating suicide in 2021 (Centers for Disease Control and Prevention, 2023b), and I'm sure that many more have considered it at some point in their lives. So seeing that someone wants to die and claiming that they have depression is like seeing somebody cough and claiming that they have pertussis.

What happens when these teachings are taken to someone with actual depression? They do not make things better. They undermine the credibility of the person sharing them and harm the causes or religions with which that person is associated. They may even cause resentment because the person struggling with depression knows that whoever shared that misinformation did not take the time to objectively research what they were talking about before passing off their "solution for depression."

When we become aware of misunderstanding because of definitions for either of these reasons, we have a couple of options. We can try to force everybody around us to use our definitions. That normally comes across as arrogant. Fabricated definitions raise red flags for a society that is very vigilant against religious cults. If they are 400-year-old definitions, that gives the impression of being out of touch with the modern world and modern problems. The other option is to simply use the commonly accepted definitions, referencing the older ones only when contextually appropriate, such as when reading older books or discussing quotes from the past. This option, though much more practical, receives pushback from people who claim that we must use the Bible words and their definitions in our everyday life to live biblically. I am not aware of any legitimate basis for that idea, but I have encountered it in my life. Your choice here affects your ability to minister to people in the modern world.

Beliefs

The other significant area of misconceptions I want to address is beliefs that are not grounded in truth but are accepted and held anyway. In reality, they are false and give us a skewed perspective on life's picture. So we will counter some of them here.

If Someone Quotes the Bible, What They are Saying Must be Biblical

Paul Washer (2019) had a famous quote that said in part, "Twist not Scripture lest ye be like Satan." The Devil got to Eve in the garden by questioning God and his Word. He tried that again with the last Adam in Matthew chapter 4, but Christ refuted him with Scriptures. So he tried a slightly different tactic in Matthew 4:6. He took a passage of Scripture and said basically, "Hey, if you do this, God will take care of you, and everything will work out fine. I even have a Bible verse to prove it. And if things do not work out, you must not really be God's Son." For a vast number of people today, if the Devil cannot make them doubt God and his Word, he will test their discernment. He promotes things that sound good and even uses the Bible to back them up. But you can make parts of the Bible say anything. Once there was a man who had just started reading his Bible. He would open the Bible, put his finger on a verse, and try to live that verse for the day. One day, he opened his Bible to Matthew 27:5: "And he cast down the pieces of silver in the temple, and departed, and went and hanged himself." Not quite certain what to do with that, he decided to try again and landed on Luke 10:37: "Then said Jesus unto him, Go, and do thou likewise." Now he was very confused, so he tried a third time and landed in John 13:27: "And after the sop Satan entered into him. Then said Jesus unto him, That thou doest, do quickly." THIS IS NOT HOW TO LEARN FROM

THE SCRIPTURES! If a person uses a verse in such a way that contradicts known truth, or if the Holy Spirit from God convicts you that the statement is not consistent with God's Word or his character, study it. It may be that what you thought was true is not. But many times it is simply a person taking a verse here, a part of a verse there, changing a couple of words and definitions, leaving out a key detail, or otherwise wresting the Scriptures to claim something that is utterly false. Just because someone claims to back up their beliefs with Scripture does not mean that it is biblical.

If a Man of God Claims He Got Something From God, it Must be in Agreement With the Mind of God on the Matter

The Scriptures are filled with false prophets, corrupt prophets, defiled priests, and other religious leaders who never heeded God. But what about those who sometimes had a good walk with God? Some are like Aaron, whom God exalted; yet he led the people into worshiping the golden calf. Or what about the unnamed prophet in 1 Kings 13? He was respected enough that the young man of God (one of only 11 people in the Scriptures called that) believed that he really had a word from the Lord that contradicted what he was told by God. The Lord apparently had spoken through this prophet in the past, and he did again later in the chapter. But in this instance, the old prophet made something up and deceived the young man of God who had just done a great work for the Lord. Destruction was the result in both cases. Corporate deception resulted in corporate destruction, and individual deception destroyed the individual. Just because an idea comes from a man of God does not negate our responsibility to do the work, study for ourselves, and go to God on the issues at hand.

Everything Ultimately Produces Good in our Lives

People believe, teach, and often use various Scriptures (Romans 8:28 is among the most common) to promote this idea. Unfortunately (or as the all-knowing God would have it, fortunately), these verses in context all refer to a future day, either in the millennial reign or the eternal kingdom. Simple common sense applied to the characters in the Bible or just the world around you would quickly dispel that notion. Many godly men in the Bible and throughout history died under great affliction, never having seen any good come from their pain personally or corporately during their life here. Even today we cannot understand the circumstances in the world around us.

Those who believe good must come in this life from all circumstances are susceptible to two major pitfalls that I have seen. One is that they get so infatuated with trying to find the good in the situation that they almost get lost in the land of make-believe. They are constantly looking for the good to come, but they are never able to locate it. It becomes a pursuit of futility for them. Others think that because they cannot find the good, somehow they must not be right with God or must not love him enough. They begin to self-criticize and self-destruct, all the while ignoring verses detailing God's love, mercy, and grace for us.

In reality, God never promises good for us in this life. It is an eternal hope in the eternal life. You may end up like Job, where your latter end is more blessed than the first. Or you may end up like Jeremiah, who suffered greatly during his life. On top of that, the people he was trying to minister to ignored him and went into captivity. The remnant left still wouldn't listen and decided to go down to Egypt. History tells us that he was stoned to death trying to minister to the remnant who went to Egypt. So much for seeing good for the suffering in his life. His faithfulness was richly rewarded with rebellion and a painful death! You can love God and still not see any good from your circumstances until this life is over.

(One of my friends who peer reviewed this portion responded that if it causes pain yet makes us more like Christ, then it is producing good in this life. I absolutely agree with that. But I believe the good being referred to goes far beyond that, such as is referenced in I Corinthians 4:17 and II Peter 4:13.)

If it Feels Good, it Must Be Good

We know that eating milk and cookies for dinner feels good to most children. Never bathing, never going to school, not brushing their teeth: all these are things that would feel good to most young people if left to decide for themselves. That is why they need someone to help them see the longer term consequences of their desires and actions and to protect them from bad decisions that they would make on their own or that others would push them to make.

As adults, things do not really change. It just sometimes takes longer for the consequences to catch up to us. In fact, it may not happen at all in this life. Some people can smoke until the day they die and outlive most healthy people. However, most, after years or even decades, begin to reap the results of their pleasure. So just because something feels good now or seems to produce good results doesn't mean that it is really good for you.

If it Hurts, it Must Be Bad

Just because it causes pain doesn't mean it is bad for you. Now, pain is bad. Most everything that causes pain does so because it does damage, which is bad. But sometimes it is still good for you. Getting poked with a needle is bad. It causes pain. It breaches the skin barrier and goes through the immune system's first line of defense. It enters the bloodstream, potentially carrying pathogens with it. It causes fear. Sometimes it takes four of us to hold a single kid down just to successfully start an IV. Despite all that, and the fact that some patients would never choose it or allow it if it were not forced upon them, sometimes it is the absolute only right thing for the patient. Sometimes the things we go through in other situations in life, even if we feel like circumstances or other people have forced them on us, are actually good for us, despite the pain and discomfort they may cause. In her book *Dopamine Nation*, Dr. Anna Lembke (2021) argued that our constant exposure to pleasures causes us to feel more pain. On the other hand, constant exposure to pain and suffering causes us to feel "overjoyed" when a form of deliverance is given. It may be that things that make us feel good are bad for us, and things that hurt us are good in the long run far more than we believe.

A practical application of this idea is evident across social media. Posts constantly mention removing or blocking "negative people." There are multiple things wrong with that mindset. Although there are times when that is the correct response, they are rare. We need adversity in our lives. We need to be challenged. It makes us better people when we reevaluate something that generated negative responses. Do we really mean it? Did we say it wrong where it was misunderstood? Do we just disagree? Is the other person even challenging us, or are we misunderstanding them? Questioning ourselves due to criticism is not always bad. Also, nearly everyone will be negative or critical at some point in their life. So we will end up very lonely if we use negativity as an excuse to cut relationships or connections, even if it feels good in the moment. Our first response always should be to try to work through problems with our critics, if they are even critics and not just friends with a difference of opinion. Most importantly, those posts reveal a selfish, wrong mindset. We only have the connection for how it affects us or makes us feel. That kind of self-focus makes us even more sensitive and is worse for us in the long run than the negativity is. If we are looking for how to bless those who curse us, it becomes hard to block them. So be careful: just because something sounds good and makes you feel good doesn't mean it is good for you in the long run. In this example, I believe you actually end up both feeling and actually being worse after the temporary pleasure.

To come to a proper understanding of both the issues at hand and the factors that lead to them, we must be able to correctly discern which definitions to use in which contexts. To do that we must know that there are different definitions and contexts and be aware of what they are. We will delve into that with more depth in the coming chapters.

Then, when evaluating the situation and outcome, we cannot allow beliefs that we have been taught but cannot be factually proven to affect our analysis. Every belief must be viewed in the light of known truth, and those that cannot be proven should not be utilized in our attempts to love others, lest we also lead them astray and cause more harm than good.

Chapter 4: The Human Trinity, a Foundational Truth as it Relates to the Mind

"And God said, Let us make man in our image, after our likeness. ... So God created man in his own image, in the image of God created he him; male and female created he them." – Genesis 1:26,27

Man was created in God's image. I've had people ask me before, "If we were all created in God's image, then why are there two genders?" Their point is that we do not all look like God, so we can't all be in God's image. But this image is not referring to physical appearance. The key reference to this image is the plural forms. God said, "Let us [plural] make man [singular] in our [plural] image [singular]." A single human has the image of a plural yet singular God. In one of the marvels of God and his image in humans, these three parts are connected and affect each other while remaining distinct and independent of one another. If you are thinking to yourself, "Those statements are exact opposites," you are correct. Opposite statements can both be true.

If you try to minister to enough people, you eventually will meet someone who has an unhealthy mind and body but a great soul and spirit that are seemingly strengthened by their physical adversities. You also will meet people who have a bad body that has become a grief to the soul and spirit. Some people have soul or spirit issues that directly affect the body. All are real. An unhealthy body does not necessarily mean a deficiency in the soul or the spirit. And healing the soul or spirit will not necessarily result in a healthy mind.

This becomes relevant because all three parts of the human trinity contribute to our mental health. Different approaches target different areas of the human being. Many attempts to minister are simply out of balance because they only focus on one part of the human while neglecting the other two. This results in incomplete results or even failure. A healthy understanding of all three is necessary to make appropriate decisions later.

The Ministers to the Physical Mental Health

Modern medicine and modern psychology for the most part deal with the physical body. As such, they are very good with the physiological aspects of mental health conditions, but they also tend to lump soul and spirit problems in with the physical. This leads to them at times trying to fix problems from a medical perspective that cannot be fixed in that manner.

The Ministers to Soul and Spiritual Mental Health

On the other extreme you have religious people who try to make all problems ones that can be fixed through the soul or spirit. I readily agree that all the problems of the mind, body, soul, and spirit are a result of the original sin. It is true that any of the disorders or challenges mentioned later in this book can be made worse by past or ongoing sins, and that stopping the sin and/or addressing it biblically can have a positive effect on the mind. However, that does not make every problem involving the mind a soul or spirit problem. Complete healing in situations regarding mental health is therefore very unlikely with a soul or spirit solution alone.

I have heard more ignorant people than I care to count make the argument that since depression, anxiety, posttraumatic stress disorder, and so forth aren't in the Bible, they do not exist. By that ridiculous argument, neither do the flu, ulcers, smallpox, appendicitis, or a myriad of other conditions that affect the human body. Still others have claimed that the Bible tells us everything we need to know about anything pertaining to life. Then they go to YouTube to learn how to change the oil in their car. If they have a broken bone or need surgery, they definitely go to a doctor who has studied and possibly even specializes in that area. But they deny the need to have doctors who study the mind.

So the two categories of people have two opposite extremes: one tries to put everything into a physiological box, and the other tries to make every problem spiritual. This attempt to cross terminology and jurisdictions makes for confusion and poor outcomes. They are both right in some situations and wrong in others. So the first area in which we need discernment is whether the problem affects the body, the soul, the spirit, or some combination of them. If a problem affects more than one part of the human being (and most of the ones I encounter do), a one-dimensional solution may provide only partial relief. When people see a partial success, it often reinforces their approach. "When you are a hammer, everything is a nail" becomes the modus operandi. They try to apply the solution they are comfortable with and have been trained in to every situation, with enough encouraging results to keep them from considering other perspectives. Often that results in the person they are trying to help having an incomplete recovery. This ultimately leads to frustration and discouragement that may extend into other areas of life and relationships.

Next we will introduce some of the challenges inherent to different parts of the being and how they affect it. For the sake of avoiding confusion, when I am writing of physiological challenges, I will use medical terms, and when I am writing of challenges to the soul, I will use biblical terminology.

Chapter 5: The Soul Impact of the Mind

"Man became a living soul" – Genesis 2:7

The Existence of the Soul

The soul is the essence of who we are. It is the result of the breath of God himself. It is the reason that we are a human "being." This breath of life from God defines us. It forms the trinity, God's image, that we were created in. It is what makes us distinct from the animals. Being from God himself is what gives us our conscience (our sense of morality) until it is seared by our actions and acceptance of a wicked society. It is the original subject of the study of psychology. It is the first part of the trinity that we will deal with here.

The first thing that we must consider when attempting to make sound decisions in matters pertaining to the soul is, "What exactly is it?" We know it is the part of the human that has the greatest intrinsic value, far greater than the body could ever have. Stop for a minute and think of the human body. What gives a body (not a person, just a body) value to you? Is it size? Shape? Muscle? Bone structure? Whatever it is, just think with me of the perfect body, one that would have more value to you than any other in the world. The soul of the most abhorrent person in the world has infinitely more value than that body. If we could grasp that and become soul-focused rather than body-focused, it would change how we view people. It would change our ministry.

This is quite amazing to think about, given how much we invest in our bodies. Vitamins, cosmetics, natural foods, healthcare: all these and more are investments in our bodies. People's bodies are bought and sold (often illegally) or rented out, but if we are being honest, nobody could ever pay what they are truly worth. The anatomy and physiology of the human body—scientist have barely scratched the surface of the study of the human brain—are thousands of times more intricate and ornate than the finest automobiles available today. A single human nuclear genome contains an estimated 3,200,000,000 nucleotides of DNA, and there is one of those genomes in approximately 10,000,000,000,000 cells in the average human body (Brown 2002)! For all that, the body loses value and eventually becomes so worthless that we bury it. People are demoralized to see their bodies in decline and devastated to see another's reach its end.

The soul, by contrast, never loses its value. It is just as precious on its last day on earth as the first. Its value is irrelevant to the body's condition. To contrast its value with the body, we know we value our body quite highly. But it was literally all made out of dirt. Our soul came into existence from the very breath of God! The soul has the knowledge of good and evil. The soul will see heaven or hell. It is our conscious existence.

The Problem of the Soul

The soul has a problem. It received the results of the fruit in the garden. The Devil told them in the temptation, "Ye shall *be* as gods, knowing good and evil" (Genesis 3:5). He knew that fruit was going to affect their soul, their existence, their very *be*ing. The knowledge of good and evil became a part of their soul when they ate the fruit.

I personally believe that knowledge of good and evil included many subcategories. You are welcome to disagree, as I do not have definitive Scripture on the topic. But you hear people say, "You can't know courage (good) without fear (evil)." "You can't know joy (good) without knowing sorrow (evil)." "You can't know peace (good) without turmoil (evil)." These statements offer me no comfort, as I do not wish to know either. I believe that I was created to be perfectly satisfied and content without ever even knowing how good I had it.

Now the distribution of good and evil is radically uneven. Some people and areas receive so much good that it begins to rot them. Some receive so little that they dry out, shrivel up, and are barren. Some receive it in seasons. For others it can change almost daily. It is never in perfect balance and always seems to cause stress. This is the effect of the knowledge of good and evil on our souls.

Recall that psychology was initially a study of the soul. *Psychopath* is a combination of two words that mean "suffering soul." The word appears to be a rather late entry to the English language. But it would seem evident to me that originally people recognized that extreme or incessant suffering of the soul could drive someone mad. This madness would manifest as a lack of care for self, others, or societal norms, or a combination of these. Even today it seems that a suffering soul can contribute to mental health problems.

Here is one example of that suffering:

> And I saw a new heaven and a new earth: for the first heaven and the first earth were passed away; and there was no more sea. And I John saw the holy city, new Jerusalem, coming down from God out of heaven, prepared as a bride adorned for her husband. And I heard a great voice out of heaven saying, Behold, the tabernacle of God is with men, and he will dwell with them, and they shall be his people, and God himself shall be with them, and be their God. (Revelation 21:1–3)

Try to imagine the scene. Satan has been cast into the lake of fire. He does not trouble us anymore. We are in God's presence in our glorified bodies. We are exactly where he wants us to be in his perfect will. We have just witnessed the new heaven and new earth. We have just seen the New Jerusalem in spectacular, unimaginable glory. The grandest announcement ever commands our attention. Yet... in verse 4, "And God shall wipe away all tears from their eyes," we are still weeping uncontrollably. This is our soul suffering still with the knowledge of good and evil.

This is not the result of Satanic oppression. This is not the result of the infirmities of our flesh. This is not because we are out of God's will. This overwhelming sorrow is not because we are in sin or because we are somehow missing God's plan for a victorious life. We cannot improve by getting in God's presence; we're already there! We can't "focus on the good things." We are literally seeing and hearing some of the most spectacular things ever! This is totally the result of (extreme) knowledge of good and evil on our souls. We are overcome with "negative" emotion. And it appears to me in Isaiah 65:17 that the only way it ends is that when God wipes the tears away, he wipes our memories at the same time. At this point, the knowledge of good and evil is taken away. Our souls are restored to their original state, matching our glorified bodies.

This account shows us truths that clearly refute teachings I have heard. One truth is that as long as there are memories, there will be burdens to our souls. It is impossible to achieve a "complete victory" over them this side of eternity. Another truth is that not being able to control your emotions does not necessarily make something wrong. "You can't let your emotions control you" is only true some of the time.

Why the tears?

Matthew 25:41

Then shall he say also unto them on the left hand, Depart from me, ye cursed, into everlasting fire, prepared for the devil and his angels:

Everlasting fire is impossible for us to understand in the limitations of this body. Everything we know is bound by time. When it comes to something as immensely painful as being engulfed in fire, that time is thankfully very brief. We either pass out or die in short order. But even with our incomplete understanding we know it is a terrible thing, and we warn people not to go there.

But there is so much more to the horror of rejecting God, for he is the source of all goodness and satisfaction. God is light. When you exit his presence you will never have enough light to see anything again - total darkness while being tormented. God is the source of relationships. Apart from him you will never communicate with another soul. All you will hear forever are the screams of the other damned. God is the source of our breath. Forever the lost will be gasping, trying to catch just one more breath. God is the source of love. You will never feel love again. You will never feel hope again. The punishment is everlasting, no chance of escape. All of the good sensations, from the taste of a sweet treat to the satisfaction of a job accomplished are forever denied. All that are left are longings, cravings, despair, depression, and both imaginable and unimaginable physical and mental torments.

Romans 9:2 That I have great heaviness and continual sorrow in my heart. 3 For I could wish that myself were accursed from Christ for my brethren, my kinsmen according to the flesh:

God loves you so much he gives you a choice. True love does not bully or manipulate. He is good to you now whether you choose to accept him or not. But he lovingly warns you of the future consequences of rejecting him and thinking you can have goodness without him. What a terrible day that will be.

There are times and situations when we cannot manipulate our emotions to elicit a positive feeling, no matter what we put around us or what we try to focus on. And contrary to popular religious beliefs, God does not expect us to. He does not tell them that they need to get over it or move on. He knows that such is not possible as long as the memories exist. Once again, these people were in God's presence in his perfect will, doing exactly what he wanted them to do and living his plan for them to the fullest. But they were still distressed, grieved, sorrowful, and more.

A third truth is that we should not always appear happy. Even when we are in God's will, certain people and situations should be upsetting. In a broader sense, the "negative" emotions we experience are not universally condemned in Scripture. Sorrow, grief, fear, and the like all have their accepted place. They are now part of our nature, and God understands that and does not condemn it. In the garden, the knowledge of good and evil was the consequence of eating the fruit. Grieving their effects in this present time is not necessarily inappropriate.

Before that we did not know either one. Things like sorrow and fear are both good and evil depending on the situation. In our current state they are necessary. The same apostle who wrote Philippians 4:4, "Rejoice in the Lord always: and again I say, Rejoice," also wrote Romans 9:1–2, "I say the truth in Christ, I lie not, my conscience also bearing me witness in the Holy Ghost, That I have great heaviness and continual sorrow in my heart." He is always rejoicing, yet having great heaviness and continual sorrow. The man after God's own heart (David) wrote in his songs about great rejoicing and victory, but also of distress and fear. There is a time and place when all of those are appropriate in a person's life. There are also pitfalls the Bible warns us about for many of both the "positive" and "negative" emotions. Amy Edwards (2022) has compiled quite a list of the emotions and their potential pitfalls in her book *Full Disclosure*.

We will now look at a few of the more common burdens directly connected to the soul.

Knowledge

Knowledge is the first mentioned good and evil burden of the soul after the fall. “They knew that they were naked” (Genesis 3:7).

Knowledge in the present is a two-edged sword. On the one hand, it helps us prepare for and minimize the effects of things such as disasters and diseases. On the other hand, it allows us to begin sorrowing over them long before they affect us. Terminal illnesses create sorrow for those who have them, their friends, and their families. Pandemics create sorrow and side effects in the body long before and after the main wave has hit, because we know it is coming or could still be out there. Sudden tragedies create sorrow for those who know of them and are affected by them.

Our knowledge has increased drastically in the area of what is available or could have been. People who miss out on opportunities with friends kick themselves for it later when they see pictures online. People who live in abusive or neglectful homes know that others out there have a better living environment. Orphans see pictures of kids enjoying time with their parents on social media. In days past, they would have known that they were missing out. But now they know far more. They can see exactly what they are missing out on. Then it hits far closer to home for them. Some people dream of coming to the United States of America because they think they know what life is like here based on knowledge they have gained online. Then they are sorrowful when they are unable to fulfill that desire. Knowing what we think we are missing, or what we know we are missing, has contributed to an increase in sorrow today.

We now live in the "information age." We have more knowledge than existed in the best universities of the past right at our fingertips. Knowledge is increasing at an earlier age. Kids today are maturing faster in every measurable category than ever before. (To clarify, some today use the word "mature" when they should be saying “responsible.” Responsibility can and should be taught, so if we call irresponsibility “immaturity,” we absolve the need for a teacher and any obligation to invest in their education ourselves. I am referring to it in its correct definition.) People are reaching puberty faster. They have more knowledge at an earlier age than ever before.

I have made this statement before and have been challenged by records of young people in past days who knew several languages. That argument is invalid for a couple of reasons. One is that any normal young person, if given the opportunity, can learn other languages alongside their first. Children who grow up in a multicultural setting often learn multiple languages naturally. That speaks more to a person's opportunities than to their knowledge. The second reason is that you cannot compare gifted children of one era to average ones of another. An average or above-average 12-year-old 400 years ago would know basic addition, subtraction, multiplication, and division. Today's 12-year-olds are multiplying fractions. A gifted child years ago might have known some algebra. I had a 10-year-old show me how to calculate pi! Calculating pi was not even possible 400 years ago!

Young people today have absorbed way more knowledge than their less technologically advanced ancestors. The average young person has a slight advantage. The significantly gifted have an immeasurably higher floor! The possibilities for learning and knowledge acquisition are now so great as to overwhelm even the most capable of children.

But this is just the beginning. Children 400 years ago learned reading, writing, and arithmetic. Today, they learn reading, writing, arithmetic, social sciences, climate engineering, privilege, and sex ed. Some of the stuff they learn as young people would give me anxiety even today if I believed it. I can't imagine being taught at 10 years old (as has happened in some places in the United States) that I might have been born in the wrong body, and the only way to fix the problem is to have extensive, painful, and irreversible surgeries before I hit puberty and then take medications with potentially severe side effects for the rest of my life!

Their knowledge from school is only the beginning, however. They learn from the news. They learn from the shows. They learn from the adults around them who do not understand that they can't yet appropriately handle the knowledge. They learn from their friends. They learn from Google. The list could go on. The knowledge they gained as a child potentially can cause problems into adulthood. Unfortunately, most adults who did not grow up in the information age do not even really understand how these problems exist, let alone the troubles they have caused.

The source of knowledge these people are educated from is extremely important when it comes to the effects of sorrow. I already mentioned that worldly peers are not great educators. Neither are televisions. They are extremely inaccurate. Depending on the audience the producer is trying to appeal to, the movies may be too sensual. They may be too gory. They may be too limited while trying to keep the content rated for everyone to enjoy, and in the process, not show things as they really are. They may be too reserved, not showing the full consequences of bad decisions, so as not to affect the viewers.

Working in emergency medical services, I cringe most of the time when an ambulance crew is on the television. It does not usually represent us and how we work well. But why would it? Nobody's life is at stake on the set. So why show any concern beyond just putting somebody on the stretcher or checking on any part of the body besides where the problem is scripted to be? I hear military servicemen do not like war movies. The television will never be an accurate reflection of any part of society, so its inaccuracy makes it a poor educator.

Also, the television is not currently designed for education. It and most of its content were designed for amusement. That means you are intended to absorb its messages and portrayals without using your brain. True education involves critical thinking. In the case of education, we should be thinking about a situation like Jesus would. When we see someone on the sidewalk smoking a joint, we have opportunities to practice this Christ-like thinking. We should ultimately be thinking about trying to bring him to a right relationship with Christ. But before that can happen, we will have an opportunity to show compassion. We do not get that with a television. The whole set is fake. Even if it were real, we cannot minister to a character on a screen. It is increasing flawed knowledge with limited opportunities to process it with the correct mindset.

Not all knowledge appears to be created equally for our souls. Knowledge involving humans can be most distressing.

Past history is not our friend. Just look at how many people are burdened because of who their ancestors were or what they did. That shouldn't bother us today, because God makes it very clear in Scripture that every individual in every generation will be judged for his own sins. But the knowledge that one of their ancestors was, say, Ted Bundy or Adolph Hitler, would cause some severe distress because we know how they treated other humans.

Others blame their socioeconomic status and lack of opportunities now on their ancestors and their decisions. In many cases, that blame can be justified. But knowledge of past bad decisions only makes the present more aggravating, and focusing on the past distracts us from seeing the real issues in the present. In many cases this knowledge has no real benefit today and only drags our sentiment down.

We know more about the suffering in the world. A few months ago, Hamas raided Israeli communities, brutally murdering some, abusing, torturing, then killing others, and taking still others hostage back with them to Gaza and abusing them there. Israeli Armed Forces responded by invading Gaza, and in the months since, thousands of children have been killed, most of the population has been displaced, and much of the country, including schools and hospitals, has been destroyed. Two hundred years ago, a dispute that minor in the Middle East would not even have been known to most of us here in the Americas. One hundred years ago, there would possibly have been some lines of text about it in the local newspaper. In modern times, the day it happened we were seeing high-definition pictures and full-screen videos of all the dirty details.

The day of the initial attack, videos from the "music festival" were already being leveraged for public support, replete with the horrors and destruction of gunfire, rockets, and tanks. Later, cameras would enter the houses where whole families were murdered, revealing blood everywhere, bullet-riddled walls, and bodies hastily concealed under sheets. With time, more graphic details and pictures began to emerge about the torture and sexual abuse that occurred during the raids.

In the days since the Israeli invasion, the media has become awash with videos of injured and emaciated Gazan children, suffering for crimes of people they do not even know or understand.

A normal person will experience sorrow from the knowledge of what the Israelis endured in the raids and of the consequences of that for their lives and families. They will also feel sorrow for the innocents in Gaza, especially those children whose homeland has been turned into a warzone.

We have unprecedented access to information and knowledge about suffering worldwide. It bothers me quite severely at times how women are treated in Afghanistan and Sudan, or how the Syrians and North Koreans are suffering at the hands of their rulers. We can see the pictures and read the articles in nearly real time. Present knowledge is increased in both amount and vividness of detail.

Firsthand knowledge appears to increase what I will call "empathetic sorrow." A soldier, for example, might have been much more distressed by our bungled withdrawal from Afghanistan and the American lives it cost than the average person. A person who has lost a child is far more deeply grieved when he hears that another has lost a child than someone who has never had kids. Someone who has been raped may be far more deeply touched by reading about sexual violence, including in conflict areas, than the general population. Firsthand knowledge would seem to increase the sorrow response to events people encounter in society every day.

Certain categories of people have greater knowledge and corresponding increases in empathetic sorrow. Soldiers have seen death and destruction in a way few have. Police and first responders see the results of the worst evils in society that most people will not ever even hear about. In the United States, these three careers have high rates of suicide, in part because people can't deal with that knowledge and corresponding sorrow.

Fear

Fear is the second mentioned issue affecting the soul after the fall. Webster (1828/1995b) defined it as "a painful emotion or passion excited by an expectation of evil, or the apprehension of impending danger." He further stated, "FEAR is the passion of our nature which excites us to provide for our security, on the approach of evil." Obviously, this one was impossible before the knowledge of evil.

Fear is another consequence of knowledge we can trace back to the fall, even before the curses are pronounced. In that instance, Adam connects it to his nakedness. That reason for fear was completely irrational because nothing had changed in that regard since the day before. They were not in any more danger to need clothing for protection. We have no indication that God was upset with their nakedness. Yet fear motivated them to make aprons of fig leaves and then hide.

So we see that fears are often misplaced. Adam was afraid because he was naked. He should have been afraid because he was sentenced to death for disobedience. Many people are afraid of falling. They really should be afraid of hitting the ground when they stop falling. Sometimes the fears we see or the fears people express are not actually the root of the problem. They are just an easy thing to apply the fear to.

Fear falls into the good and evil category. “The fear of the Lord is the beginning of knowledge” (Proverbs 1:7); that is good fear. “The fear of man bringeth a snare” (Proverbs 29:25); that is evil fear. Sometimes it is just plain practical: “The lion hath roared, who will not fear?” (Amos 3:8). In my opinion it is quite sensible to fear at the lion's roar. It leads you to take appropriate precautions and preparations. In many cases, fear in my life leads me to be more diligent in my preparations than I might be otherwise. But it can also have very negative side effects. It can produce effects in the body such as paranoia or anxiety. (On the other side of the coin, medical paranoia is also very good at producing irrational fears. Do not assume one causes the other without thorough investigation.)

Sorrow

Sorrow the third mentioned (Genesis 3:16) and last insinuated (Revelation 21:4) affliction of the soul. Noah Webster (1828/1995d), in his *American Dictionary of the English Language*, defined sorrow as "the uneasiness or pain of mind which is produced by the loss of any good, real or supposed, or by disappointment in the expectation of good." Sorrow and fear appear to be the two goods and evils most closely associated with knowledge. This is a massive, far-reaching, pervasive influence on our mental health.

How is sorrow both good and evil? "For godly sorrow worketh repentance to salvation not to be repented of" (good), "but the sorrow of the world worketh death" (evil; II Corinthians 7:10). Sorrow can motivate us for good. Broken people are among the sweetest and most compassionate in the world, especially toward those facing similar heartbreak. Years ago, a mainstream school of thought held that God could more effectively use broken people in ministry and that causing sorrow was one of the key ways God broke people. Broken people now often feel like they can't be used, when in reality they are often better fit for ministry than ever before. But the world's sorrow is destructive. Judas is a classic example of that. He was sorrowful and reacted opposite to God's will. He killed himself.

With knowledge, sorrow appears to have come. God tells the woman he will greatly multiply her sorrow. He doesn't say that he will give her sorrow. I do not believe it existed before the fall. It appears to have begun with the knowledge of good and evil and been multiplied by the curse. When God curses the ground and tells Adam that he shall eat of it "in sorrow," it appears to me that he is simply acknowledging that sorrow came with the knowledge of good and evil. Notice how both humans had sorrow referenced, but the serpent did not. The serpent was living in a sin-cursed world of suffering and pain, but without a soul, and without the knowledge of good and evil, he does not experience sorrow.

Consider this to drive home the point that the knowledge is what brings the sorrow. Two hundred years ago, if someone moved to California and died, it would have taken weeks for the news to reach family in the East. The family did not start mourning when the person in California died. They started mourning when they received knowledge of the death after the letter was delivered weeks later. The more and sooner we have knowledge, the more sorrow we have.

Ecclesiastes 1:18 indicates a direct correlation between knowledge and sorrow: "He that increaseth knowledge increaseth sorrow." We were called out on the ambulance for a 2-year-old who died in her sleep.

She was dead for hours and had no hope of revival, so our job was to help monitor the family while waiting to give a report to the coroner. The mother was extremely upset. She understood exactly what had happened. The 5-year-old sister had no idea what all the commotion was about. She knew mom was upset, and she was trying to comfort her mom and make her smile. She did not know, and her mom could not make her understand, that the little sister would never return to this world. Mom was sorrowing because she knew. I was sorrowing more than the 5-year-old sister was, because she did not possess the knowledge. (I'm honestly tearing up writing about it. Sorrow persists as long as the knowledge exists. But I'm not upset about still being sensitive. I would much rather be a crier than be calloused and unfeeling toward the pain of others.)

One final thing to note about sorrow is that the Bible states the man will work in sorrow, but the woman will have sorrow multiplied. I believe that women experience more sorrow than men in life. Some have tried to tie that increase to the pain of childbirth. I disagree. If there is a connection between the sorrow and conception parts of the curse, I think it is more likely connected to the increased rate of the menstrual cycle than it is to the pain of childbirth itself. Vijayakumar (2015) in her journal article pointed out that women with postpartum psychosis had a 7-fold increase in suicide risk for the 1st year after childbirth and a 17-fold increase long term. We have seen that hormonal fluctuations can have a significant effect on the body, and it could well be that the body and its infirmities in this case are affecting the soul. Consider that women are twice as likely as men to attempt suicide (Vijayakumar, 2015). Roughly 57% of adolescent girls felt persistently sad or hopeless, twice that of boys their age (Centers for Disease Control and

Prevention, 2023a). Those numbers are significantly worse than before the pandemic. The effects of social isolation and increased exposure to the ills of technology seem to have affected them especially. Even before that, there was an underlying difference in the data between the genders, which I believe can be traced back to the curse in the garden itself.

Desiring Death

Wanting to die is another affliction on the soul. It is heavily stigmatized in part because of certain religions. In an effort to keep people productive in the systems they were enslaved in, both to the church and to those who financed the church, they taught that anyone who committed suicide went straight to hell with no hope for redemption. That is heretical. In their teachings, just thinking about suicide was a sin that needed to be confessed. I speak from experience when I say those thoughts may come. They are not always a sin. Like many unpleasant thoughts, what you do with them and how you entertain them are very important to keep you from harming yourself and others.

When I say "what you do with them," I am not talking about dismissing the thoughts as quickly as they come. Job told his friends about them. Elijah expressed them to God in a serious conversation. Paul wrote about them in a letter to the Philippians. Sometimes we need to work through unpleasant things. Alistair Begg (2002) said in a *Truth for Life* audio broadcast, "A Christian mind is not one that is trained to think only about Christian topics. It is a mind that has learned to think about everything from a Christian perspective." I believe the statement could not be any more accurate or applicable to our topics here. Sometimes we need to ask where the thoughts came from. Are they straight from the Devil, or did something else trigger it? Many times, I have seen that when someone attempts or commits suicide, it triggers similar thoughts in others who care about them. We might ask if anything or anyone helps when they are there? What might the thoughts turn into, and how do we keep them from getting worse? Sometimes they are just a passing thing, and sometimes they need more serious interventions. By the way, if Job, Elijah, and Paul all wanted to die at some point in their lives, that's pretty good company.

Before I actually get into the circumstances surrounding Elijah's and Job's desires, I did want to note that it is easy for Christians today not to want to die. We can now say, "Oh, I can't wait for Jesus to come back" or "I sure hope the rapture comes soon." In most cases we do not hear that because the people really love Christ's appearing. If that were the case, they would be a lot more like the apostles, acting crazy as they tried to get everyone to go with them in the little time they had left. No, most of those people just want to escape this world with all its troubles, this body with all its sicknesses and pains, their bill collectors, and their hurting relationships. It just sounds more spiritual to say "I wish Jesus would come" than it does to say "I wish I would die."

Elijah had an interesting situation. He had prayed for a drought. For 3 years there was no rain. At the end of that time, he challenged the prophets of Baal and of the groves to a duel of sorts. We all know how that went down. If not, you can read I Kings 18. In the end, 450 prophets of Baal died, the Israelites declared that the Lord was God, and there was a great revival. Except that there wasn't. The powers that existed were still in control of the national religion, and God had no intention of forcing a change through terrible acts of his greatness. (Elijah wanted the wind, the drought, the fire, and the earthquake, but God doesn't force people like that. He uses a still, small voice to invite them.)

So Elijah was confused and disappointed, and his life was in danger. It wasn't just any danger. There was an enraged queen after his head with even more fury than during the previous 3 years of headhunting. He ran for his life, left his servant in a more friendly country (presumably so he wouldn't be in danger from association), and continued his flight. He then asked God to kill him.

He was alone, confused, disappointed, and feeling hopeless. Here is why I disagree with the idea that he was depressed. He still had tremendous mental clarity, and his reasons for wanting to die were perfectly rational. This is not what I experience in my conversations with depressed people. Depression is an irrational psychological issue. People I talk to with depression usually do not know why they want to die; that is just how they feel. Elijah very clearly wanted God to kill him so he didn't die by Jezebel's hand. Whether it was because of Jezebel's well-known reputation for torture and cruelty, or because he thought Jezebel getting revenge would undermine what happened on Mount Carmel, or a combination of both, we will never know. But his capstone argument was basically that God needed to kill him or else it was likely that Jezebel would. (Ironically, to this day he still hasn't died!)

Despite the issues that oppressed his soul, he still made good decisions: turning to God and obeying when God eventually gave him instruction. He also learned from his experience. The next time we see a monarch trying to cut his head off, he called down fire from heaven to burn up the soldiers!

Job was a rich man, until he wasn't. On top of that, he lost his family. All of his kids were killed, and his relationship with his wife was strained. He developed painful boils all over his body. Then his friends who came to visit him turned out to be terrible for him at that time. (On a side note, his friends were still his friends. Although they did him wrong at the worst possible time, they thought they were helping. Just because your friends hurt you when you are down doesn't mean they are not still your friends. In the end, God gave special care to making sure that Job's relationship with his friends was restored, emphasizing how he thinks about it.) He felt alone, like even his friends had turned on him. He was confused and disappointed in life. He actually thought he and the world with him in it were worse off at that point than the day he was born. And he felt hopeless. He thought he was terminally ill and didn't understand how he wasn't dead yet. Despite all that, he submitted to God's will, even when he couldn't understand.

Most of us will experience times in our lives when we feel alone. We will get confused and disappointed. Circumstances will seem hopeless. We will be mentally and physically pained. We may be afraid. People may be angry at us. Every day might seem to be causing more trouble and dragging out the inevitable. We will wonder if the world would be better off without us. In those situations we must trust a wisdom higher than our own. He will take us out of it in his perfect plan and timing.

Grief

Grief is one of many less-mentioned afflictions of the soul that we find after the banishment from the garden. Webster (1828/1995c) defined it as "the pain of mind produced by loss, misfortune, injury, or evils of any kind; sorrow; regret." In Scripture, it often appears to refer to situations in which one's mind (will, intent, or plan) is frustrated by circumstances beyond one's control. In Ecclesiastes 1:18, it is proportionate to wisdom, which makes sense. Wisdom allows you to make good plans for yourself and others. Grief comes when they are unable to be completed. In the Bible this can be due to rebellion, death, or a simple lack of ability. When we talk of grieving after the passing of a loved one, it is because we willed for them to live. In our minds we had plans and desires for them. Many times it is good that we want to come to pass. But they were frustrated and unable to be born out.

The common thought of grief is connected to when one has experienced a loss, such as death, which results in an upsetting of plans. But grief is also experienced from loss resulting from wills that never materialized. An example of this is found in 1 Samuel 1. Hannah was grieved because she was barren. She had no opportunities to fulfill her plans and desires and felt a loss as a result. I can sympathize somewhat with Hannah. I've willed, intended, and planned to provide for a family by making physical preparations. I've prepared to protect a family through education and training. I've wished for a wife whom I could show how she means the world to me and for someone who would love me enough to choose me over everyone else in the world. By now I could have kids, with ages in the double digits, preparing to make an impact on the world and do more than I could ever accomplish myself. They could see an example of someone who loves God and catch hold of that desire to love God and to share his love with the world around them. But I am grieved, not for the wife and kids I had and lost, but for the family I intended to have and feel a loss.

Many experience grief because of a loss that is visible which cuts off obvious plans. But many more experience grief because of an unseen loss, such as Isaac and Rebekah when they found out that Esau married Hittite wives. It appears that their hope for him was to not marry a local, and they were grieved when it happened.

Care

One more soul burden will I bring out. There are dozens more in Scripture. I just wanted to give a few examples. This burden is care. Webster (1828/1995a) defined it as "charge or oversight, implying concern for safety and prosperity." We care about many things, most of them good things. Note in the garden that Adam was not to care for it as we see with other lands later, but to keep it. At that point, there was no need to care. There were no threats to safety, and prosperity was assumed. In fact, the first time the word is used in Scripture, it speaks of God's care for the land he promised to Israel. But cares can become a burden that affects our spirit and body. Martha was an example of this in the Bible. She was doing a good thing serving, but it affected her relationship with her sister and her Savior, and it burdened her body.

Care has been incorrectly translated in some modern versions as "anxiety." As a result, verses like Philippians 4:6 would be understood to declare that an anxiety attack is a sin. However, there is a distinction. Anxiety is a physiological impulse that we will discuss more in the next chapter. Care is a rational choice.

So we can see these soul burdens have been received because of the knowledge of good and evil. They have in some cases been enhanced by the curse. Often they have a good origin or cause. They can have good or evil effects on us in life. We must use discernment when considering these things.

Chapter 6: The Physiological Impact on the Mind

"To get a concussion, you need a brain." John Cena (2003, as cited in DoubleZWWE, 2021)

The physiological component is the current focus of most mental health conversations today. With few exceptions, mostly from people who read the Bible and apply antiquated definitions to today's terminology, most conversations about the mind are going to refer to the brain and the hormones that affect it.

The human brain is a marvel of creation. It has an estimated 86,000,000,000 neurons making roughly 100,000,000,000,000 neural connections (Caruso, 2023). That is obviously a lot of opportunities for good or bad things to happen. These neural pathways can be reinforced by repetition, allowing the connections to run more quickly. They can be damaged by trauma, chemicals, hypoxia, and many other things that also affect the rest of the body. Plaques can accumulate, restricting or occluding these pathways. The neurons and their connections alone make mental health a highly complex field of study.

The brain is divided into right and left hemispheres. Beyond that, it is divided by scientists into many other lobes or regions, depending on the type of behaviors being studied. Many will divide it into three key areas, with the central area controlling life instincts and some emotions. The middle part is the action/reward center, where habits are formed and addictions are processed. The outer region is where our logical thinking and expression reside. The brain can be subdivided into many levels further based on the specific functions and processes it controls. The resources are distributed from the center outward. Consequently, when there is a deficiency, the core survival needs are met first, and the processes related to logic and critical thinking suffer first. (This is part of the reason people who teach self-defense want it to become a trained reflex. It moves the maneuvers out of the thinking area of the brain into the habit area, allowing it to remain more accessible for longer.) Generally speaking, if our brain is prioritizing due to deficiency or adverse influences, the part that makes rational decisions and knows why we do what we do suffers or even stops first. This inherently means that our ability to control our actions suffers. Which part of the brain is being used is also a complex study that factors into a person's mental health.

Over 50 hormones in the human body cooperate with the brain to influence the rest of the body. We think of them as controlling mood, but they also regulate homeostasis, metabolism, growth and development, sexual function, and sleep. They can vary in ratios from hour to hour and complement or conflict with each other and the rest of the body. Once again, whole fields of science are devoted to studying this aspect of our physiology. I am just giving an overview so you can try to understand the many complex areas that can be damaged or fail, contributing to a decline in mental health.

(These hormones are a good representation of the balance we have for what we can and cannot control in our body by our willpower alone. Certainly we can choose actions or behaviors that can raise or lower our blood pressure, but any control we think we have in that area is very limited. In my personal experience, the histamine (hormonal) response to eating food that I am allergic to influences my blood pressure far greater than any conscious thoughts or actions I take for it. The correct response for this imbalance is not to will my body into submission but to take a pharmaceutical antihistamine (usually diphenhydramine hydrochloride) to stop its effects, or take another hormone (epinephrine/adrenaline) to counter the histamine effects.)

Beyond the major categories, many other physical factors affect our brains. One example is the presence of toxins (such as ketones) in the bloodstream. Accidental or intentional overdoses affect the mind. Even gut bacteria, body temperature, and system pH all play a role.

Opposition

There is some pushback against the current study of mental health sciences. The following are a few regularly used arguments opposing it.

This Study of Modern Mental Health Is Relatively New

The term "psychiatry" was coined in 1808, 12 years after the first vaccine was developed. The first modern publication on "diseases of the mind" was released 4 years later. Various "ailments" were studied and defined to some extent during the 19th century, a period that also saw our first use of anesthesia (1846), commercial contraceptives (1886), and synthetic opioids (1898). The oldest disorder that is still in use by the same definition and name today is Alzheimer's disease, discovered by Alois Alzheimer when he performed an autopsy on the brain of a deceased patient in 1901. Many of the disorders have been cataloged much more recently, such as posttraumatic stress disorder in 1980 and chronic traumatic encephalopathy in 2002.

Because it is so new, there are not many indisputable opinions on the topic. The diagnoses are nearly always based on behavior, because we do not yet have a good alternative. Electron scans of the brain and other brain-mapping technologies show promise in this area, but more research and testing are needed. Some disorders still can be confirmed only by a postmortem autopsy, such as posttraumatic stress disorder and chronic traumatic encephalopathy.

Also, because it is a relatively new field in medicine, we do not have much long-term understanding of the outcomes of our treatments. My personal opinion is that we are overusing some psych medications, much like opioids were overused in our recent past. Opioids helped meet a need and were regarded for years as good with minimal side effects. If there was evidence of harm, it appears to have been buried by money. Now that we have seen the long-term harm they cause, we, as a society, regret giving them to so many people. I anticipate the same future for many of these medications we are prescribing today without having seen the long-term effects.

It Is Rapidly Changing

We have mind-affecting chemicals today that did not exist 40 years ago. Depression and other mental health disorders are listed as potential side effects for an alarming number of over-the-counter and prescription medications (including, ironically, those designed to augment mental health). Social media and its side effects have gone viral. Radiation (also called electromagnetic frequencies or EMF) and blue light from cell phones and other screens are everywhere. Both Dr. Brewer (2021) and Dr. Lembke (2021) mentioned in their respective books that even junk foods like potato chips have been researched and developed to more strongly affect dopamine levels in the body, altering brain function. If even our foods are engineered to negatively affect our mental health, it is no wonder so many people have disorders today! The world is changing so rapidly that the field of medicine cannot keep up, and no area is changing faster than the one affecting our brains.

It Had a Less Than Appealing Start

Sigmund Freud (1856–1939) is sometimes called the Father of Modern Psychology or the Father of Psychoanalysis. He was a Jew by heritage and an atheist by profession. Because of his background and the fact that many of his writings were considered humanist and crude, many religious people have painted all of psychology with an offensive brush. (Every medical work I have read could be considered crude to varying degrees by nonmedical people. In most medical works there is far more weight given to accuracy and clarity than to societal pleasantries.) But another Jewish man who believed in "Spinoza's god" (Albert Einstein) gave us the foundation for the atom bomb. Ideological differences and heritage do not negate truths, no matter what level they are on.

Although many of Freud's ideas are now regarded by modern psychologists as debunked (Stewart, 2018), he recognized and widely disseminated the idea that unseen scientific forces beyond the control of the human will factor into psychological diagnoses. This transformed that field of study as radically as Einstein's Theory of Relativity did physics. I am sure, much like any scientific idea conceived before detailed records were kept, that he was not the first scientist to propose such a concept. He just happened to be the one who disseminated it at a time society was willing to listen.

It Contradicts Some People's Ideas of Human Will

I know there are some of the opinion that a person never has physiological problems that cause him to act beyond his control, or beyond the control he should have if he were right with God and following biblical principles. I passionately disagree.

I have seen men who got dementia and thought they were back in the war. Christian men were vulgarly cursing an unseen enemy and hiding behind their beds for fear. Paranoia was so great that even the lamp might be hiding an improvised explosive device. I have seen a man who suffered a traumatic brain injury who had the belligerence of a man wholly intoxicated and could not be reasoned with. I was told he was normally mild-mannered and easy to reason with otherwise. I have seen multiple people with advanced urinary tract infections whose response to the toxins the bacteria in their bodies produced was to get completely naked. Normally at their age they would have a somewhat refined sense of modesty. I cannot begin to describe to you the wide range of mental effects chemical overdoses, both intentional and accidental, have had on otherwise good people. I have seen even blood sugar issues cause both children and adults to be out of their right mind.

(In the case of a child, fear of punishment was successful at gaining temporary focus and compliance. But things would have been far more effective and appropriate if they had recognized that something was wrong physiologically and gotten the blood sugar under control. Also, you have not lived until you have tried to stick the finger of an angry, metabolic, overweight, 7-year-old. You had better be sure that kid can't move a muscle the first time, because you'll need a miracle for a second chance. You learn very quickly that people get superhuman strength when they feel a needle!)

Furthermore, what evidence does one have, biblical or otherwise, that such factors do not exist? The absence of a direct mandate to address them does not mean they do not exist. God never tells us how to repair an airplane or treat cancer, either. But airplanes and cancer are both very real. And despite no direct commands on how to treat it being given, it is referenced several times in Scripture with the Old English word "madness" or being "mad." Obviously our definitions, the words we use, and our understanding of the condition have changed greatly over the last 400 years, but you can see that those words appear to refer to mental challenges. It can be brought on by drunkenness (Jeremiah 51:7) or oppression (Ecclesiastes 7:7). It can result in poor judgment (Proverbs 26:18–19) or incoherent talk (1 Corinthians 14:23). These are by no means exhaustive. David faked madness (which seemed to be a readily recognizable ailment in that time and place) while in Gath (1 Samuel 21) to escape the consequences of killing Philistines before he fled there. During Paul's trial before Agrippa (Acts 26), Festus suggested that Paul was mad because of the strange things he had been claiming to have seen, heard, and done. We can gather from the interactions recorded with David, Nebuchadnezzar, and even the maniac of Gadara that people deemed insane were separated from society as much as possible.

The obvious question is, if there are times that we cannot control our actions from a rational or spiritual perspective, how do we know when a person can or cannot? I can't tell you. I believe that is an individual judgment call and there are no one-size-fits-all answers. Cookie-cutter solutions are easy to produce and market, but they aren't usually the best option for unique people in life, ministry, or healthcare. So I am not going to give you one. I hope to arm you with the knowledge necessary to make an informed judgment. At this point, we just need to be aware that those situations exist.

It Is Mostly Unrecognized in History

I believe that there are three main reasons that we do not have many historical records of mental health.

- **Relevance.** Aside from a few monarchs who developed mental problems during their reign (King George III of England being possibly the most famous), not too many madmen did anything worth recording. They were never put into positions of leadership for good reason, contributed little to society, and were consequently little thought of or recorded.

- **Recognition.** If you were to read materials from centuries ago, you would eventually find people trying to perform exorcisms on patients exhibiting symptoms that look very much like indicators for dementia. People who came home from war and became grumpy or explosive in their personality would now be understood to be suffering from a form of posttraumatic stress disorder. At times you may read of a sickly child who was always fussy or angry and eventually died when the sickness was in the house. Those kids could have had diabetes. (I am aware that diabetes is a disease involving the pancreas, but untreated blood sugar issues affect the mind and leave people agitated, incoherent, and in severe cases, unresponsive.)

- **Child mortality.** In some cultures, deficient children were not even allowed to live. In others, the lower standard of healthcare meant that children who have survived because of modern medicine would never have had a chance even 100 years ago. I can't even begin to count the number of diabetics (mostly children but some adults) who got sick with something like the flu, got dehydrated, let their blood sugar get too low, and would have died were it not for interventions from ambulance and hospital personnel. Just look at the number of babies in neonatal intensive care units across the country. We are able to help many more children to survive than in times past.

Abraham Maslow (1943) postulated a hierarchy of needs (often arranged as a pyramid) in his paper, "A Theory of Human Motivation." He believed that certain levels of physiological needs must be met before we can consider psychological needs. Using that theory, when most of the country were sustenance farmers, we did not devote a whole lot of thought or resources to mental healthcare. We have come a long way in our studies and understanding. We have no excuse to still be trying to exorcise dementia patients.

Major Disorders

We have established that the physical mind greatly influences, and at times even controls, our physical body independent of our will. Let us look at some major disorders a person can be diagnosed with today. For the most part, this will be a concisely modified paraphrase of some definitions from the fourth edition of the *Oxford Dictionary of Psychology* by Colman, with occasional personal thoughts included. I understand some of these definitions will change with time, but they are good for now.

Alzheimer's Disease

Alzheimer's is a degenerative brain disease. As mentioned, it is the oldest condition in this list, having been discovered in 1901. It is a form of dementia. The two major symptoms are loss of memory and emotional instability. It is usually terminal, leading to death in 4–12 years, and can be definitively diagnosed postmortem by the amyloid plaques and neurofibrillary tangles (affecting the neural pathways) in the brain that are visible during the autopsy. We currently have few options besides pharmaceuticals to treat these people and help with their quality of life until they eventually pass (Colman, 2015a).

Anxiety

Anxiety is a state of uneasiness that includes both the feeling of uneasiness and bodily symptoms from the tension. By itself, it is not necessarily a bad thing. Harriet Lerner (2004) has a whole chapter in her book praising it. David Livingstone (n.d.), both a Christian doctor and missionary, included it with the afflictions of sickness, suffering, and danger as a physiologically introduced trial that could affect the soul and spirit. He seemed to regard anxiety as a problem from the external as opposed to one originating from within. It moves into the disorder territory when it becomes "excessive" or "largely uncontrollable." At that point, it is usually classified by its triggers and the types of symptoms it produces. Generalized anxiety disorder has no specific trigger and symptoms such as "restlessness, tiredness, difficulty concentrating, irritability, muscle tension, or sleep disturbance causing significant impairment in everyday functioning" (Colman, 2015b).

We have taken patients to the hospital just to get them out of a situation that was causing anxiety. I have transported patients who have voluntarily been institutionalized in a mental health unit instead of going back to a bad situation. I feel for these people, as I know how much I despise those places. Yet they believe it is still better than the situation that they are in. Is this the best thing for these people? It definitely is not. Is it good for our healthcare system? No, it is overworked as it is. Obviously, the best course of action is to remedy the living environment. But we can't do that. And as healthcare workers, we are not going to leave a person in a situation that will result in their destruction. So we do the best we can with the options we have: institutions, therapy, and medications.

This aspect of situationally induced mental health challenges seems to be getting worse. As housing prices rise, fewer people can move out of bad situations. This contributes not only to the challenges caused by the environment but also to additional stress from feeling trapped. This is prevalent among young adults, but even more so among teens. Society keeps teens trapped by restrictive laws. No longer can you move out at 14 and get a job at a canning factory. (I know someone who did that over 70 years ago.) You can't even afford rent on two full-time minimum wage jobs today, if they could even find an employer who would offer them just one! So people end up stuck in a bad home environment or moving out into a bad, but in their mind slightly better, communal environment. I understand that the laws were implemented to protect some children from bad situations. But this protection deprived others of the ability to escape bad situations. Young people just do not have those opportunities or that freedom today. So we take them to hospitals with anxiety attacks. They go to mental health facilities for weeks at a time and do not want to go back home. We do this because their options are limited and they must try something.

Attention-Deficit/Hyperactivity Disorder

This disorder is characterized by "inattention, hyperactivity, or impulsivity, causing problems at school or work and in the home, and interfering significantly with social, academic, or occupational functioning" (Colman, 2015c). This is possibly the most controversial mental health diagnosis out there, not in the least because it is very broad, and because after the Individuals with Disabilities Education Act started providing federal funding for schools to accommodate these disorders, the number of students diagnosed with it drastically increased. In my opinion, there likely is a place for it and medications targeting it, but it also appears to have been overdiagnosed.

Chronic Traumatic Encephalopathy

This degenerative brain disorder is caused by repeated impacts to the head, often associated with contact sports or settings with concussive blasts. Symptoms of the brain damage often do not show up until years after the injuries. Depending on the area of the brain damaged, it can alter a person's mood, cognitive functions, or even ability to sleep. It can be definitively diagnosed postmortem by an autopsy of the brain (Colman, 2015d).

Depression

Depression is a "mood, state of sadness, gloom, and pessimistic ideation with loss of pleasure in normally enjoyable activities" that in severe cases can be accompanied by a number of other related symptoms (Colman, 201e). It is a symptom of several different depressive disorders.

Paranoia

Paranoia is a general term for a variety of delusional disorders in which a person has a nonsensical suspicion. What the person suspects is happening and how they react to it further classify the type of disorder (Colman, 2015f).

Posttraumatic Stress Disorder

Posttraumatic stress disorder is a

> trauma- and stressor-related disorder ... arising as a delayed and protracted response to experiencing or witnessing a traumatic event involving actual or threatened death. serious injury, or sexual violence to self or others. It is characterized by recurrent, involuntary, intrusive, distressing memories of the traumatic event or dreams related to it; flashbacks causing the individual to feel or act as though the trauma were recurring; intense distress and physiological reactions in response to anything reminiscent of the traumatic event; persistent avoidance of the stimuli associated with the trauma; a numbing of responsiveness and heightened arousal, manifesting as insomnia, irritability, difficulty in concentrating, hypervigilance, or exaggerated startle response. (Colman, 2015g)

This disorder has a wide range of causes and symptoms, so I fclt it was important to give you a great part of the definition to fully appreciate the scope.

Psychosis

This is a very generalized disorder encompassing many more specific diagnoses, with the predominant symptoms being delusions or hallucinations. Depending on the context, it may be caused by pathogens, chemicals, or other factors, or it may be solely a mental disorder (Colman, 2015h).

Traumatic Brain Injury

This results from external force, usually in a single incident. The symptoms depend on the area of the brain affected and the severity. A traumatic brain injury can leave people moody, handicapped, incoherent, dead, or many other things in between.

Disclaimer

These diseases are real and recognized. But just because these diseases exist does not mean that I agree with every diagnosis or every treatment plan. Some of these criteria are relative, similar to the pain scale we use on the ambulance. Every patient may rate the same pain differently, and ultimately we must use our best judgment when administering pain medications. Likewise, what causes a "significant impairment in everyday functioning" is also relative.

In general, I believe that certain conditions are overdiagnosed and overmedicated. But imagine for a minute that you are in a position where someone has come to you for help, and you want to help them. You have no objective way to measure how serious the problem really is. Your decision is based on subjective criteria, coupled with a desire to help, a desire to appear compassionate and listening, and a need to maintain the relationship so that if this treatment doesn't work out, the patient still trusts you enough to come back and get it fixed. Until you have been in that situation, you have no idea the challenges these doctors face in their specialties.

I believe that there are three classes of medications that are overprescribed and have the potential to create dependencies: pain medications, hormonal regulators (commonly though possibly inaccurately called birth control pills), and psychiatric medications. I am very sympathetic to the prescribers in all three cases. They have no objective data for how bad the problem is, they are sympathetic to personal problems they may never have experienced, and they want to help. The challenge gets even greater when you are dealing with kids. They cannot communicate well. They often come in with a parent who doesn't know them that well. They may only be there because of a referral from a teacher who sees something "wrong" in class. In those cases the provider has even less information with which to try to help than in most regular cases.

There is also the Rosenhan effect, a very famous example of a study in which diagnoses went very wrong! Doctors could not distinguish between actual patients with mental challenges and pseudo patients who merely reported having symptoms to get admitted. Sane people were being forcibly medicated at institutions, which was and is highly concerning. Even without that extreme, people may be diagnosed and treated based on their reporting and not because they actually need medications. Some may be making up a story, while others simply do not fully understand their symptoms and may accidentally mislead the practitioner.

At times, circumstances lead to medicating perfectly normal behavior for the situation. I recall transferring an 8-year-old boy from an emergency room to a longer term facility for behavioral issues. He had been institutionalized (in my opinion many of these institutions are worse than prisons) five times in 2 months. What was the trigger? He was removed from his home, he and his sister a year younger than him were separated, and they were placed in the foster system 2 months earlier. So now he is exhibiting normal behavior for the situation, which is unacceptable for the classroom. Unfortunately, it is impossible to treat the root causes of things like this. Many challenges arise when children are separated from one or both parents for any reason. We must try to help somehow. So people try to treat the results of that trauma. But the question arises, if we are medicating normal behavior for the circumstances, what are the results of applying mind-altering drugs to normal minds? I do not think the public really knows, but we are in the process of finding out.

Nondisorder Factors

Besides the actual disorders, other factors can affect our brain and our will. We already mentioned the innocuous potato chip, but many everyday items and occurrences have either a positive or a negative effect on our mental health. Some of these effects from other factors are temporary. Some recur in cycles. Some are pattern-use effects. Others are acute in origin. Some are predominantly found in one temporal category, but depending on how they are used, they may be found in another in certain individuals. These effects can be positive or negative. We will look at a few examples of each. First, let us look at an example that spans multiple categories.

Stress

Stress is an enemy of all parts of the human body. It can originate from physiological, emotional, or spiritual stimuli or any combination of them. It can come from obvious sources or the unimaginable. We know that deadlines can be stressful, but what about eating ice cream? Depending on your personality and biochemistry, your body may work harder to recover from the ice cream than from the deadlines. Regardless of the source, it can affect us at every level, from the molecular (some would argue even subatomic), to the mind, to mortality. In limited duration, stress can generate a positive effect on the body, but chronic stress tends to have a universally ill effect. Stress can impact a large number of hormones, and hormones directly impact our mental health, so it is not hard to see the connection.

Hypoxia

This is too little oxygen. In the short term, it can create a monster, quite literally. With longer durations, the person can acquire what is called a hypoxic (low oxygen) or anoxic (no oxygen) brain injury. With these types of injuries, the survival instincts are the last to go, and I have seen people live in a mindless coma due to severe ones. Death is the most severe possible result from anoxic brain damage.

Blood Sugar Irregularities

Whether blood glucose gets too high or too low, it can produce a mental state that is angry, depressed, combative, and eventually comatose or dead if too extreme.

External Sensory Stimuli

Certain stimuli can improve or strain one's mental state temporarily. Music is a great example of this. Certain songs and rhythms can be soothing or energizing. Others can be used for psychological torture, as the late Manuel Noriega (1934–2017) found out! Fingernails on a chalkboard are another example of auditory stimuli that can affect one's mind. Different fragrances that stimulate the olfactory sense can influence one's mental state. These sensory stimuli are initially temporary in their effects, but they can become chronic if encountered on a recurring or habitual basis.

Chemical Exposure

To state the obvious, chemicals, no matter how they are introduced, can affect the mind. I have seen everything from prescription drugs, to pesticides, to fertilizers have an adverse effect on people's mental states. Ketamine is a very useful example of this quality in a chemical, but others do not have any positive effects. The severity and duration of the effects is quite diverse depending on the chemical exposure and the route by which it was exposed (inhaled, injected, ingested, or touched).

Timing of Effects

Physiological factors that affect the human mind show up at various times for multiple reasons. Some are easier to predict and to mitigate than others.

Intermittent and Regular Onset

Some influences recur at regular or irregular intervals. Some hormonal fluctuations are predictable. Others have sporadic triggers or flare-ups. I expect that everyone reading this book understands that the monthly menstrual cycle has a significant effect on those who experience it. But what you may not realize is that many endocrine disorders are also cyclical, such as cyclic Cushing's syndrome. Much medical information is available on endocrine disorders, both regular and irregular, if you care to do more research.

Environmentally Based Triggers

Other recurring influences are environmentally based. For example, depression is known to increase significantly in areas that during certain times of the year have no sunrise or extended periods of rain in which the sun is not seen. And I am in agreement with the roughly 81% of mental health workers who, from firsthand experience, believe that the full moon makes people crazier (Francis et al., 2017), even though the research does not currently back that claim up. People have been observing this behavior for millennia. In fact, it is where our word “lunatic” comes from, “luna” meaning “moon.” Seasonal and environmental allergens generate a histamine response that disrupts the normal sleep cycles and hormonal balance. So there are definitely recurring factors to be aware of.

I am aware that seasonal allergies are not likely to make a person crazy or suicidal. You may wonder why I am including seemingly trivial influences in a book like this. Well, there are two reasons. One is because I believe in being a good steward of this body. If allergens are affecting it negatively, we should do what we can to minimize those effects. This could include steps such as running an air purifier, taking antihistamines, or getting hypoallergenic pets. The second reason is that I am all for buttressing the areas we can to reduce the strain on the whole physiological system. You may never be able to recover from posttraumatic stress disorder. But it is easier to deal with just the effects of posttraumatic stress disorder than it is to deal with them being compounded by seasonal allergies and the added stress that histamine response brings to your physiology. In modern times when even our potato chips are out to get us, let's use the science and technology we have to assist us in our efforts to glorify God in our bodies.

Usage-Based Influences

Some substances are used in such a way that they become patterns or habits. Obviously chemicals, legal and illegal, responsibly used or abused, can fall into this category. (This includes secondhand marijuana smoke, which I believe is negatively affecting a growing number of our child and adolescent population.) So can technology use, sex, exercise, or anything that affects us physiologically and becomes a habit. Some are simply addictions. Others have been shown to damage the brain in the long term. Obviously, try to form good habits and weed out the bad ones, because they can have a profound influence on your mental health and your life in general.

Sudden Acute Factors

Then some influences come on suddenly and have temporary to lifelong effects. Overdoses, brain or endocrine injuries, strokes, diseases, and more can temporarily, permanently, or even fatally affect someone's mental health. They can be intentional, accidental, pathogenic, or degenerative. Most of these would be considered medical emergencies. Any unexplained or sudden change in someone's mental state should be examined by a licensed doctor.

The physiological mind is a wonder of complexity, with manifold factors that can affect it for good or ill. It plays a huge role affecting our mental health.

"Now when Jesus was risen early the first day of the week, he appeared first to Mary Magdalene, out of whom he had cast seven devils." – Mark 16:9

The spirit component is definitely the component that I know the least about. It is the only one I have not personally struggled with. I hope never to. But I have had patients who struggle with this area, and the Bible certainly speaks of it. So I will share what I do know and not speak beyond that.

I do know that evil spirits are very real. Most people do not want to hear this, but they are active in our country. I have had a number of patients who I believe were possessed. Beyond that, there were more who were communicating with spirits, familiar and otherwise. It is quite comforting to know in those situations that "greater is He that is in me than he that is in the world" (1 John 4:4). It makes a person uneasy, but I have no reason to be afraid. You can expect to eventually encounter someone under their influence in your life.

Direct Influence

Spirits can exert influence either through possession or attacks (also called oppression). I do not believe that a saved person can be possessed by unclean spirits. That can only happen to people whom the Holy Ghost does not indwell. But it is very clear biblically that wicked spirits have fiery darts that fly through the air to attack Christians and must be blocked with a shield of faith. So spirits can have influence on the mental health of both the saved and the lost.

Possession

Possessed people can present with many symptoms of other physical and mental disabilities. Consequently, medical personnel often try to treat them as physiologically impaired. People who communicate with spirits get diagnosed with auditory and/or visual hallucinations. Yet my impression from the ones that I have been around is that a large number of them aren't hallucinating. Society at large likes to believe that our only interactions with the supernatural are through the Christmas wizard in the red suit and Casper the friendly ghost. But there are far more sinister forces at work.

I have had people as young as 8 on my ambulance who told me they talked to and could see their dead relatives. This young girl said that she most frequently communicated with her uncle. The most frequent problems reported from these communications across all the patients I interacted with were that the spirits would tell them to hurt or kill themselves, to hurt or kill others, or to go into the dark woods and never come back. This was true across all ages, but children seemed more likely to admit to talking to things the medical world believed were not real. Often these people received a medical diagnosis of psychosis with audible or visual hallucinations.

Sometimes the only indication of spiritual influence may be a "sense" you have that something is wrong. Most of my experience has involved other indicators from the patient. Among them are claims to interact with devils, claims to interact with deceased people, stating that one sees spirits or shadows, and claiming that spirits or voices are telling them what to do. I have heard from coworkers of instances where the person speaking even claims to be a devil talking, usually in a strange voice.

The Bible tells us much about this topic. People afflicted ranged from children (Luke 9:42) to old men (1 Samuel 28:15). They can cause a huge range of symptoms including fear and terror (1 Samuel 28:20), superhuman strength (Mark 5:3–4), blindness (Matthew 12:22), loud verbalization (Mark 1:26; Luke 9:39), muteness (Matthew 12:22), crying (Mark 5:5), self-harm (Mark 5:5, 9:22), foaming at the mouth (Luke 9:39), inexplicable pains and bruising (Luke 9:39), infirmity (Luke 13:11), and probably more that I've missed. In my encounters, there often has been a connection or attraction to darkness or death.

The child in Mark 9 would in our day possibly be diagnosed with manic/depressive (bipolar) disorder. But the Scripture clearly indicates that this was a spiritual issue, not a physiological one. Over 10 years ago I had a coworker who was diagnosed as manic/depressive. She was not much older than me at the time, maybe early 20s. She was involved in "white magic" (which is terminology the Devil uses to try to make witchcraft more palatable). At times her pupils would change color. Even at that point, knowing very little about the world around me or the spiritual realm in a practical sense, I wondered if her bipolar tendencies were a result of spiritual influence.

The maniac in Mark 5 could be identified as psychotic. Many times with psychotic people there are physiological influences from drugs. Throughout history, drugs and witchcraft often have been intertwined. In fact, the Greek word translated as "witchcraft" or "sorcery" in the New Testament was often *pharmakeia,* which has an etymological connection to drugs, medicines, and poisons. In a number of those situations, there might have been influence from both physiological and spiritual sources.

The solution to spirit possession problems only has one answer. Sensational exorcisms leave a person as described in Matthew 12:43–45:

> When the unclean spirit is gone out of a man, he walketh through dry places, seeking rest, and findeth none. Then he saith, I will return into my house from whence I came out; and when he is come, he findeth it empty, swept, and garnished. Then goeth he, and taketh with himself seven other spirits more wicked than himself, and they enter in and dwell there: and the last state of that man is worse than the first. Even so shall it be also unto this wicked generation.

Trying to rid the spirit problems may clean a person up for a time, but it also leaves them empty. Then the problem comes back worse than before. The only solution is the power of Jesus coupled with the indwelling of the Holy Spirit to take up the space previously occupied by devils. This can only be accomplished when a right relationship with God is had through salvation.

Oppression

The attacks on the mind, which also may be called oppression, may take multiple forms. The Devil is called a tempter, an accuser, a deceiver, and more. Some of the battles that take place in the thoughts, especially in these areas, could be the result of spiritual attacks. They may lead to soul challenges that directly affect a believer's mental health.

Indirect Effects

Then there are indirect effects of spiritual influence on the Christian's mind. Seeing evil and its effects—suffering, grief, pain, death, and eternity without Christ—causes sorrow, grief, and other soul challenges. Being in a spiritually dark part of the globe, even if the attacks aren't personal, can have a negative effect on your mental health.

There is a physiological component to these influences. People sometimes report feeling tension in the air. Sometimes the sounds, sights, or smells associated with serving the Devil directly affect our senses. For example, human sacrifice is often associated with evil spirit or devil worship. I have never seen it, but I have heard pain and terror, seen death, and smelled burning human flesh. I would definitely imagine being around something like that could cause multiple negative stimuli. These negative stimuli are transmitted to the body, causing stress and other negative emotions. The resulting response from the body and mind often tends to a decline in mental health. Constant exposure would cause stress, and that stress would negatively affect other parts of you.

Although I have little personal experience dealing with spirits, I know that they can have a great impact on mental health.

"If you can't say something nice, don't say nothing at all." – Thumper in *Bambi* (Hand, 1942)

Honestly, one would be stupid to apply that principle to every aspect of life and conversation. But I wish people would try that a little more often, because I know so many people who have been damaged by inappropriate responses from Christians. We should not just rush out without some personal preparation.

Run Some Checks

Check Your Motivation

A good litmus test for our response is found in Romans 15:1-2: "We then that are strong ought to bear the infirmities of the weak, and not to please ourselves. Let every one of us please his neighbour for his good to edification." What we are about to say, does it please us because we just must get something off our chest? Does it please us because we are encouraging someone else to live up to our standards for their life? I realize that not every conversation is pleasant for the recipient. But I believe I can make a very strong biblical case that those conversations are never pleasurable for us either. In many cases, we feel even worse after they are through. If the conversation pleases us but does not benefit the recipient, "do not say nothing at all."

Beyond this, who are you trying to help? Ask yourself some questions.

Are you trying to help them? Why? Are they a nuisance to you and society? Do you pity them? Do you have a familial or other connection that creates an obligation? Do you love them? Do you love Christ and believe that he would have you try? Is it just natural human compassion, as the Samaritan seemed to exhibit?

Are you trying to help others? Maybe they have a family that is suffering because of their struggles. Maybe they are harming society when they give in to their baser desires. Maybe someone asked you to intervene and try to help them. Maybe you see their family in pain and want to alleviate that.

Are you trying to pad your own image and ambitions? Are they another number for your ministry logs? Does assisting those lowlifes inflate your ego and sense of superiority? Is this a stepping stone to another ambition? Is it expected of you and your ministry position? Are you being paid or expecting other personal benefits from it?

Your reasoning for attempting to help someone will affect how you approach it, how much endurance you have in it, how others see you and possibly Christ through you during it, and ultimately, how successful you are. But take heart: even if you start with the wrong motivation (and I hope you do not), you can always get right and improve from there. God can even restore the time you did things wrong because of your wrong motivation. That study is outside the scope of this book, but there are times when he does and times when he does not. So definitely check your motives in prayer before you begin and during each encounter.

Check Your Preparation

I realize that not everyone will have gone to school to become a public servant, where they were exposed to destruction caused by the horrors of sin and taught how to respond professionally. In fact, some people reading this book might have been raised in a very sheltered environment in church and been mildly traumatized the first time they heard a curse word. Ministering to people who have mental health problems could make some people very uncomfortable. Some may have the idea that a Christian can never think or talk about sinful topics. That cannot be true to minister in a sin-affected world. Recall: "A Christian mind is not one that is trained to think only about Christian topics. It is a mind that has learned to think about everything from a Christian perspective" (Begg, 2002). In your preparation, you first must learn to think about everything as Christ would. All of us find sinful devices and topics (such as adultery, demon possession, and self-righteousness) to be unpleasant and distasteful. But if you cannot control your reaction to that discomfort, you stand a good chance of making things worse. I have seen benign events (possibly slightly embarrassing but completely harmless) turn traumatic for an individual simply because of others' reactions to them.

If you show embarrassment while listening to a person, they become embarrassed talking to you about it. That is part of the reason we are taught to keep a professional demeanor when talking about reproductive issues and the like on the ambulance. It does not necessarily damage a relationship or worsen the situation. But it does make it harder to help a person with the issue at hand when they suddenly become too embarrassed to continue the conversation or omit details that are harder to share.

Scorn and mockery are exceedingly damaging to the person and the relationship. If your reaction shows scorn, contempt, or disgust, you hurt that person and your relationship with them, and you make it harder for the next person to help them with the problem. If you mock them, their problem, or their coping method, you will get similar results. Do not let your reaction make the situation worse.

Causing shame is a sure way to shut down opportunities. People have different ideas about what knowledge is appropriate to share in different settings. Some people's ideas or level of discretion may not match those of the person trying to help them. But shaming them for that difference, especially if there is no reason for them to know otherwise, not only hinders your ability to help them, but also makes it much less likely that they will seek help from someone with your values or ideals in the future.

Rejection, and the fear of it, are probably the most damaging to relationships. James tells us, "Confess your faults one to another, and pray one for another, that ye may be healed" (James 5:16a). In some cases we aren't seeing healing today simply because we are afraid to confess our faults to one another and pray for one another. What fear holds us back? None other than the fear of rejection. It takes many forms. We may be shunned. We might lose opportunities to minister. We may become subjects of gossip. While at times there may be a need for some changes, in most cases, acceptance, assistance, and strengthening or restoration should be the focus.

A good example of thinking like Christ is found from our Savior himself when they brought him the woman caught in adultery. Their accusation, that she was taken "in the very act," was meant to conjure a vivid word picture. Jesus does not shrink away in embarrassment at the plainness of speech. He does not lash out because of the accuser's choice of words. He does not communicate rejection to the woman caught in one of the most abominable sins in Scripture. (Adultery is mentioned more times in the Bible than any of the soapbox or politicized sins of today.) He calmly communicates truth. His goal is restoration. She leaves knowing mercy and love. Whether or not she ever got saved is a matter of debate, but there is no debate on what happened that day. Everywhere Jesus dealt with unpleasant topics—from a woman with an issue of blood that all of society deemed unclean to a boy who tried to drown himself and burn himself alive because of demonic influence—and they never seemed to faze him.

(If you find pleasure in sins, Romans 1:32 has strong words for you. There is a difference between meeting people where they are at because you love them and enjoying hearing about or seeing sins. These things should break your heart, not be a source of satisfaction, no matter your reason. If they do not, you need to get right with God.)

Check Your Information

"If you can't say nothing intelligent, don't say nothing at all." (I just made that up.) Well-intentioned people who are trying to show Christ's love to others can still do much harm if they do not know what they are talking about, yet come across as though they do. I have seen that and hope this book will reduce those occurrences.

One of the biggest challenges with regard to information is simply ignorance. Spoken ignorance on a topic can hurt the cause of Christ as much as words spoken with malice. The Dunning-Kruger effect (in simple terms, having so little knowledge in an area that you do not know that you are not an expert; Kruger & Dunning, 1999) seems common in this area among Christians. It actually seems to be common in many areas, almost as if some people believe that being a student of the Scriptures makes them an expert physician, psychiatrist, judge, law enforcement officer, and auto mechanic.

Trying to claim knowledge and authority you do not have in a situation can harm three areas. It obviously can harm the reputation of the person who is faking expertise. Even if the recipient never knows the person isn't real, others around with more knowledge on the topic will call him out and warn their friends about him. If this person claims his authority comes from the Bible or presents his position as representative of Christ and Christians, the cause of Christ also takes a hit. Christianity comes across as disconnected at best, arrogant and ignorant at worst. The worst damage may be to the person subjected to the ignorance. If this person believes what is spoken, it can have an unhealthy effect on how the person views themselves or their problems. If they eventually realize that the spoken positions were wrong, they can become bitter not only toward the counselor but also toward Christianity in general or a faction of it. So if you do not have reliable information on what you are talking about, if you have never studied it, keep your mouth shut!

At times our information is dated. Many of Sigmund Freud's hypotheses are no longer regarded in modern psychology. We no longer perform lobotomies on people. Circumstances in facilities are slightly improved from the days of *One Flew Over the Cuckoo's Nest* (Forman, 1975). So please do everyone a favor and take just a few minutes to check whether what you are opposing is still relevant, or if you are fighting ghosts of practices and ideas past.

Sometimes our information is biased. Emergency medical technicians are probably not the best people to ask for advice on getting a pool or a trampoline. We never get called out to situations with a trampoline or pool where the people are enjoying healthy exercise as a family. We only get called out when somebody gets hurt or drowns. So we tend to hate them. Sure, hundreds of thousands of people use them to get quality rest and relaxation. Millions probably use them for healthy exercise. But we only see the ones who get hurt on them, so our perspective is skewed.

If you are in counseling and everybody you talk to has been hurt by social media, you might think that all social media use is bad. Some might think that the whole internet is dangerous with only a downside. They never stop to consider that without it, our whole commerce system would crash.

These biases are easier to see in other people when they seem disconnected from reality on a given topic. But we must be aware that we have some too. Try to get a balanced perspective before counseling others from a skewed viewpoint.

Check the Situation

Different situations may merit different truths for application. Two opposing statements can both be true. For an example, see Proverbs 26:4–5. In fact, in religious circles much strife and confusion have been caused by people taking one side of truth and trying to discredit the opposition. The most common such example may be the sovereignty of God versus the free will of man. Many truths have been applied incorrectly by looking at a portion of the Scriptures (in some cases, just a single verse here and another there, without context), conjuring a principle, and trying to apply it to all of life's situations. These people never consider that the opposite truth may be appropriate in some of those situations. Many times they even get defensive of their position and offensive toward the other, which is also a biblical truth. For example, later in this book, I talk about casting our burdens on the Lord. Then I talk about bearing one another's burdens. Then I talk about every man bearing his own burden. I will back up every position with Scripture. But we get into trouble when we take the verse to cast one's burdens on the Lord and try to apply it to every situation that has a burden, including those that must be borne alone. This indicates pride or ignorance on the part of the one misapplying Scripture. It creates confusion for the one who cannot cast his burden because it is one that must be borne alone. He begins to wonder if he is out of God's will or in sin because the burden just cannot be cast. Once again, if you are not sure or have not studied the situation and all the possible biblical truths that may apply, be very careful what you say and how you say it.

Remember the Goal

We are trying to show compassion through Christ-like love. "By this shall all men know that ye are my disciples, if ye have love one to another" (John 13:35).

It is difficult to overstate how many people I have tried to explain the love of Christ to them, with the acceptance and purpose he offers, only to receive a blank stare. They have never seen anything like it in their lives, and most of them are unwilling or unable to believe that this Jesus, whom they have never seen, will offer it to them. The places where they should have seen it are lacking, and they are suffering as a result.

Possible Examples of Love

God gave several examples for us to see love. They were all meant to show a picture of his love toward and relationship with us. But they have been corrupted by the fall. Let us look at some of these representatives and what has happened to them.

Love should start in the home. As the divorce rates show, the majority of homes in the United States have one, if not both, parents who love themselves more than everyone else in the household. Of the remaining families, many more see their love tied to how they behave, how "successful" they are, or what they do compared to what their parents would like for them to do. Unconditional love is a dream scenario. So this idea (a God that loves them unconditionally and infinitely) is a hard concept to understand.

God designed the husband–wife relationship to picture his love and commitment. In fact, his standard for how a husband was to love his wife was compared to how Christ loved the church and gave himself for it. If you study how much Christ gave to become human and then to sacrifice himself, it is an incomparable standard. But as all the infidelity, bouncing around to whomever will give you the most, divorces, and selfishness among singles show, this picture has become very flawed as well.

God definitely wanted true love to be visible in the church. In fact, God specifically stated in the Scriptures that he did not want two things feigned in the believers: love and faith.

The early church was known for its love. Tertullian (ca. 160–230 A.D./1885), in his second-century letter to Roman authorities, *Apologeticus*, made the now famous claim,

> But it is mainly the deeds of love so noble that lead many to put a brand upon us. 'See,' they say, 'how they love one another,' for they themselves are animated by mutual hatred: 'how they are ready even to die for one another,' for they themselves will sooner be put to death.

Clement of Alexandria, in his *Miscellanies*, described Christians of the same period this way:

> He impoverishes himself out of love, so that he is certain he may never overlook a brother in need, especially if he knows he can bear poverty better than his brother. He likewise considers the pain of another as his own pain. And if he suffers any hardship because of having given out of his own poverty, he does not complain. (Clement of Alexandria, ca. 153–217 A.D./1867)

Unfortunately, the Christian leaders of today are known for getting rich! Beyond that, churches' propensities for hatred, strife, envy, pride, and condemnation are all better known qualities in many congregations than love right now. In 1976 Warner Brothers released *Ode to Billy Joe* (Baer, 1976), in which the protagonist stated, "No man can be ordained as a Baptist minister unless he's ready to think the worst of his congregation." I do not endorse the movie in any way, but it shows the public perception of churches and their leaders at the time. That perception does not appear to have improved recently. That is in stark opposition to being known and even hated for a willingness to impoverish oneself, and if need be to even lay down his life for the least of his congregation!

The Corinthian church was too accepting of sin within the congregation, so Paul had to write them a letter outlining a handful of things that were unacceptable among church members. Now churches seem to have swung the other way and have been known to reject people over petty stuff. Stories abound of Christian leaders taking advantage of their positions for their own benefit, even to the harm of their people.

A large number of people have left churches over the last 50 years. Many of them parted ways simply because they could not find the positions their church taught in the Bible, and their church was not willing to accept them if they came to a different conclusion or held a different position.

If those who grew up in church were rejected because they wore different clothes or listened to different music, how is a lost, broken person ever going to see Christ's love in that church? How are they ever going to believe that the church would accept them in their current condition, when those who grew up there need to change minor things to be accepted back?

There are both doctrinal (Galatians 1:9) and moral (1 Corinthians 5:11) reasons to separate from others who claim to be believers. But those should not be the churches' primary reputation or focus. One could easily believe that the churches today have added much to the biblical list of necessary causes for separation or church discipline to the detriment of our emphasis on love and reconciliation.

I believe God has a remnant in many denominations that seek Christ first. They are consequently able to show his love to the world, like the Samaritan, even if their worship is not perfect. But in every denomination that I have been exposed to or been a part of, the majority of churches and leaders fall woefully short. Personal pride, selfish agendas, peer acceptance, financial considerations, traditions and dogmas, cliques, organizations and structure, and many more distractions have become the focus of churches, clouding or even destroying their reflections of the love of Christ.

The distractions become idols to the congregation. You cannot threaten Jesus. But you can be a threat to any idol. Threats do not receive love. They receive, at minimum, rejection. Consequently, diverse (not dangerous, just different beliefs or focuses) people are unwelcome at many churches.

So love may not exist in the family, it is flawed in relationships, and it is becoming hard to see in the average church. Sometimes, none of the communities in your life have an example that will model biblical love. It becomes harder to demonstrate what we have never seen.

Personal Hindrances to Love

On the individual level, several hindrances to practicing true love exist. Bitterness, wrath, strife, and other works of the flesh are direct impediments to knowing true love. If you try to show what you do not know, you are often exposed as incompetent or a hypocrite.

Assume Personal Responsibility

It is incumbent on us to make a change. We cannot use our upbringing, the state of religion, or our own incompetence as an excuse to go with the status quo. The lawyer for whom the parable of the Good Samaritan was created attempted to do just that. He wanted to use the current religious laws to justify himself.

But how can we remove deeply seated hindrances in our character and abilities? Our preparation, motivation, and all of the related factors in our flesh are corrupted and selfish. It is through becoming more like our example in Christ that we are more ready to show love to others. It is a process of every day learning more of him, then thinking, speaking, and acting more like him.

How can we change to manifest something that we have never seen and do not know what it looks like? To this, we find the answer in the Bible. Every time you read it through, if you are paying attention, you can see a new aspect of God's love in how he deals with his children. As we see this perfect love (and we will never exhaust its facets in this life), we can begin to emulate it in our lives. We are also given a basic description of it in 1 Corinthians 13. It is not self-serving or self-inflating. It focuses on others despite the inconveniences and even injuries it might cause to you and those you love.

What good am I now?

I Corinthians 1:4
Who comforteth us in all our tribulation, that we may be able to comfort them which are in any trouble, by the comfort wherewith we ourselves are comforted of God.

Our society has become rife with making excuses for why we can't or aren't. Disabilities, heritage, physical characteristics, our upbringing, and life's experiences are all used to limit our potential. But we serve a limitless God who works opposite to normal thinking.

Where the world says "I'm injured, I'm weak. I'm not able or fit for this task." God's principles say, "That's where my comfort and strength can work through you best."

In the past this was commonly understood. Prominent Christians declared the potential of broken and hurting vessels. Charles Spurgeon (1859, 1890, 1906) stated "...whenever God means to make a man great, he always breaks him in pieces first." "God is chiseling you ... making you into the image of Christ." "None can be like the Man of Sorrow unless they have sorrows too." "Our infirmities become the black velvet on which the diamond of God's love glitters all the more brightly." A. W. Tozer (1955) wrote "It is doubtful whether God can bless a man greatly until He has hurt him deeply."

In modern society, you need to be strong, nearly perfect, well educated, and well endowed to minister to others. Consequently, the ones we look to for help are often the least able to assist. Then the rest of us think, "If he can't help with all his abilities and advantages, how can I when I'm barely keeping it together myself?"

The truth is if you are weak and hurting in an area, it is likely where God's strength and comfort can shine through you the greatest! You should not hide because you were hurt. You suffer to be better able to serve!

II Corinthians 12:9 And he said unto me, My grace is sufficient for thee: for my strength is made perfect in weakness. Most gladly therefore will I rather glory in my infirmities, that the power of Christ may rest upon me.

> Charity suffereth long, and is kind; charity envieth not; charity vaunteth not itself, is not puffed up, Doth not behave itself unseemly, seeketh not her own, is not easily provoked, thinketh no evil; Rejoiceth not in iniquity, but rejoiceth in the truth; Beareth all things, believeth all things, hopeth all things, endureth all things. (1 Corinthians 13: 4–7)

In addition, when we get saved, the love of God is placed in our hearts. It is so great that we naturally want to start sharing it with others. It begins to flow through us to all around (Romans 5:5). As long as we live after the Holy Ghost, he will guide us in showing this love to others.

When you start approaching the unapproachable, exposing yourself to risks, loving despite considerable costs and sacrifice, and so forth, people will think you are crazy! The risk is too high, and we are too vulnerable to stop and try to help the helpless who aren't even looking for assistance in a land of wild beasts, thieves, robbers, and murderers. The cost is too great. The people are insufferable. We do not know if we are making a difference or ever will make a difference. So why stop and try to help somebody whose outcome will probably not change? We are likely just delaying the inevitable anyway. We do it because God loved us enough to take a chance on us, and now his love through us reaches out to our neighbor! Regardless of the outcome, it is always a good investment. We must let the love of God abound in us and through us despite the outward pressures. This will make your religious peers uncomfortable. But it will be readily noticed by everyone that you are different, operating under different motives. And this compassion will make a difference for some.

Chapter 9: Recognizing Opportunities to Love

"But a certain Samaritan, as he journeyed, came where he was: and when he saw him, he had compassion on him, and went to him." – Luke 10:33–34a

With roughly 1 in 5 people in the United States suffering from a mental health illness and roughly 1 in 20 living with what is considered a serious illness (Substance Abuse and Mental Health Services Administration, 2021), they are literally all around us. That does not mean that there are multitudes who want or need our help. There are some who are beyond our ability to help and need professional medical assistance. Others may still be in denial of or defensive of their difficulties. They are obviously not yet half dead.

We Must Notice the Need

Remember, in our example parable, the man who was injured and lying beside the road was "half dead." He was unable to ask for help. Therefore it was incumbent on the people walking by to notice, be oblivious of, or even ignore the man and his condition. I would guess that most of you have not been around hundreds of mental health patients, seeing them at times in their natural environments, talking to them, and listening to their stories. To a degree, at this point I instinctively recognize some of them, and it goes far beyond the people who are overtly acting crazy.

There are a few "red flags" that alert me to a person for whom a compassionate touch may make a difference. Remember, that is all we are doing. We are offering compassion. We are not offering therapy. We are not trying to treat a disorder. We are simply trying to make a difference in the lives of hurting, suffering people through compassion. Many people who are suffering or struggling do not get much of it in today's society. But it is something that I have seen even very heavily medicated people respond positively to. When you couple that with the fact that numerous people with mental struggles turn to self-destructive coping methods that the righteous in society despise, it is even harder to recognize them and for them to admit to being hurt. They hide until they are too despondent to care. Recognizing and responding correctly to these visible indicators is a step in being able to show compassion.

Self-Harm

An incident of self-harm is one of the visible opportunities to show compassion. People are very critical of this, and some will even use it as a reason to institutionalize a patient. So some will try to hide it and start cutting on their bellies or thighs instead of visible areas. Some will bruise themselves or deliberately enter situations where they know others will harm them.

There are three reasons I commonly hear from these people. Sometimes it is a visible expression of the hurt they are feeling on the inside that nobody else can understand. People may not understand that method of expression either, but at least they can see that something is hurting, something is wrong. Second, it can be a distraction from the mental pain. There are different levels to this. In extreme cases I have talked to a couple of people who told me they would cut themselves before getting in bed, because it was easier for them to sleep distracted by the pain the razor blades caused than it was to sleep with the pain of their thoughts. Third, some people have told me that they self-harm because they feel like they deserve it. This is why the majority of the people I talk to put themselves in situations that they know will hurt them.

Many have similar feelings that they just do not usually take to the level of self-harm. One nurse I met in the aftermath of the COVID-19 pandemic told how she would constantly sit or lie on the floor next to the trash can. Between the stress of the ridiculous hours she was working and the strain of losing so many patients to death, her mental health was affected in such a way that she subconsciously felt like she belonged with the trash. She said she did not even realize that was why until she got professional help. The vast majority of people who share these feelings with me are similar in that the reasons they feel this way are usually beyond their control. Yet they punish themselves for things for which they are not culpable.

There are two main ideas that I have encountered repeatedly. One is that they feel they need to be punished for failing to protect a family member or friend. That unnecessary guilt becomes a driving force for seeking pain and punishment to make (unnecessary) retribution. But the guilt never leaves. I imagine people who have legitimate guilt from a major event would face stronger, more pervasive challenges. I am unaware if I have ever encountered people with that guilt. The other idea is that they were robbed of their self-worth. Sometimes it is from sexual violence, sometimes from unrelenting criticism, and at times from rejection by people who should love and accept them. The result is feeling unworthy of anything better than the pain they are experiencing, and that they should seek out pain and punishment appropriate to their perceived value. As a reminder, our value comes not from our actions, not from our bodies, not from our connections in this world, but from our soul and its value in relationship with our Creator God.

Words

Another noticeable opportunity is the words people say. Because topics like these are distasteful in society, they are often raised as jokes. Any time people talk about depression or especially suicide, I take them seriously, no matter the form or context. I try to let them know that I value them, and God values them even more. If it is an appropriate setting, I will try to ensure they know that help is available and that there are several options. I ask my coworkers if they know what the suicide hotline number is (988 in the United States as of this writing) when it seems appropriate. Listen to people and the words they say.

Self-Medication

You may notice people who are self-medicating. I am not talking about people taking medications prescribed by a doctor. I am talking about drugs, alcohol, and other medications that may not have been prescribed. Almost anyone who is using illegal drugs is challenged mentally. If they use them long enough, they will do severe damage to their brain.

Even marijuana has been linked to psychosis in adolescents with developing brains. (Once again, that can happen even from secondhand inhalation.) Alcohol was the original antidepressant. It is mentioned by a king in Proverbs 31. It obviously is used today for a lot more than that.

If someone admits that they are using any of these to alter their state of mind, that is a pretty good indication that they are self-medicating. Because of the effects of alcohol and drugs on the physiological mind, these people often need professional help. Before you say, "The Bible has all the answers we need to help people with these addictions," use that

Bible to keep someone with delirium tremens alive. Until then, I strongly suggest professional medical care for these people.

Changing Identities

A very obvious opportunity to show compassion arises when I see people trying to change their identities. This can be anything from trying to use a new name, to radically transforming their looks, to trying to become a new gender. A new identity is often an indication of a hurting old one, coupled with the thought that the new one will bring acceptance or a fresh start. It rarely does. The old pain is still there, coupled with new pains from some old friends not fitting well with his or her new identity and from the rejection accompanying the change. I get particularly concerned when I see someone who has tried to adopt a new identity but subsequently let it fall into a state of disrepair. That kind of despondency after such a passionate and radical attempt to improve life sometimes precedes something drastic. Similar to the people who talk of suicide, I try to let them know that I care about them, not for their identity, but for who they really are, their soul, and that God loves them for the same reason.

We Must Make Contact

So the question becomes, if you see these red flags, do you just walk up to people and ask if they are OK? I do, yes. But I am probably not the best person to be writing this portion. I grew up home-schooled and went from there to a small Bible college. So I do not have much of a foundation for what is accepted in regular society. The year after I graduated, I went to emergency medical technician school where I lost my sense of shame with regard to trying to help people.

So I really do not have a clue what a "normal" person would, could, or should do. But I'll tell you what I do, and you can take it for where it is coming from.

I try to show everybody I meet that I care about them, from the cashier at the gas station to the person I pass on the sidewalk. (To that end, I almost never use a self-checkout. It is a missed opportunity to interact with a person.) If I see one of those red flags, I definitely ask if the person is OK. Sometimes they think I am just being courteous. I might get a little more specific. "You look a little down today," or "I see your arms are cut up, and I care. I just want to make sure you're alright right now." I have seen people who appear to have tried a new identity that did not work out with things in their shopping cart that concern me. I do at times approach them to check on them. "You look like you've had a rough go of it lately. I work on an ambulance, and I've seen people get hurt with some of that stuff in your cart. I just want to make sure you are OK."

It may be that I have a God-given sixth sense from trying to help so many of these people during my career. It may be God just protecting one of his socially naive children. But I have never had somebody get upset with me for asking if they were OK. I noticed, which shows a certain level of care in and of itself, and then I put forth the effort and took the risk to check on them. In my experience it has been universally appreciated. Sometimes there are opportunities to minister further. Sometimes it has opened the door for spiritual conversations at a later encounter. And sometimes I believe I just helped a person to keep going long enough for God to send someone else their way. I am not necessarily recommending it this approach. I am just sharing my experiences here.

Regardless of how God leads you to approach somebody, it is obvious that the battered, bloody, half-dead man in the ditch is never going to jump up and approach you. If you do not find a way to make contact and initiate a connection, you will not have the ability to show these people compassion.

When you see the need and make contact, you find out if there is an opportunity to go farther and show compassion by loving that person. That person could be anyone from a random stranger to your best friend. Remember that in a half-dead state, even your best friend will not be able to reach out to you for help. So be alert and looking for opportunities, even among those closest to you.

Chapter 10: Loving in the Acute Phase

"The first step is always the hardest." – ancient proverb

We have up to this point been given a lot of information. Now what do we do with it? Is the person we want to help physiologically incapable of making good decisions? Are they fighting some kind of spiritual battle? Are they temporarily depressed, or is it a chronic disorder? Are there soul factors at play? If there are, are they healthy or not? This chapter covers what to discern and how to respond in the beginning stage.

Pray

If you haven't already, you need to pray. It is definitely worthwhile to stop for a minute and ask for wisdom and direction from the Lord. It would be even better to keep an open line with him all day. But occasionally we forget, and unexpected or intense situations can return our focus to him. Proverbs 3:6 tells us to acknowledge God in all of our ways, and he will direct our paths. I believe that would apply to how we try to minister to people. So definitely do not think you can go it alone.

Approach

Whether you approach someone or they come to you for help, the order is still relatively similar. We start most conversations in a courteous manner, with hellos, introductions, and so forth. I admit friendly conversations out and about are far less common now than they were before COVID-19 was used as an excuse to be afraid of everyone around us. The fear of contagion got us to stop standing close and conversing with each other. We became accustomed to setting stuff down on the checkout counter and then stepping back away. Masks hid facial expressions, making communication difficult. But I feel like the fear of contagion morphed into a fear of interaction that continues to this day. Be a rebel—be friendly.

During the initial approach and interaction, you should notice if the conversation seems incoherent, if the responses or speech seems inexplicably slow, or if something else is off that might indicate an immediate medical problem. On the ambulance we use four questions to determine if the part of the brain that makes rational decisions is working well enough to make their medical decisions. We want to know if the patient knows who he or she is (by asking some form of "What is your name?"), where he or she is (city, address, or some other appropriate question and answer), what time it is (year, day of the week, or time of day), and what is going on ("What are you doing?" "What happened?"). If the person seems off, I try to work those types of questions into the conversation.

If the answers are inappropriate and the person is unaccompanied, I try to get them an evaluation, either by calling an ambulance or by finding a person who knows them. I try to see if this is normal for them or if they can take the individual to a doctor. I have tried calling the adult social services in Arkansas to get people help without burdening the ambulance and emergency room services, but they told me they only collaborate with the hospitals. So in most cases here, when I meet somebody who doesn't know where they are or where they are going, and can't tell me what happened or even what month it is, my only options are either to leave them or to call an ambulance. With my experiences with brain injuries, overdoses and other poisonings, and even blood sugar issues, I can't in good conscience just leave somebody like that. These issues can degenerate and even become fatal. We have resources in today's society (whether you like it or not) that can provide them with an assessment and make certain they are getting the medical care they need.

If at any point you feel that you or they are in any kind of danger, leave the situation and contact emergency services. You cannot help anyone if you are dead.

If they are alert and responding correctly, by this point they know I care about them and want to help. If they want to continue conversing, my next two inquiries are usually "What/when did you last eat?" or "Are you eating well?" and "How are you sleeping?" These questions have two coordinated purposes. First, they indicate that I care about the person I am talking to. Some people do not even understand their soul, but they understand that if I care about their body, I care about them. Second, just because the part of the brain that makes rational decisions is operating does not necessarily mean it is functioning well. If one or both of these are contributing to the problem, they are a simple fix. And once they are functioning at their peak, we have more capacity and momentum to tackle possibly more complex problems.

When you first encounter the person you are trying to minister to, do not overanalyze. In the acute phase, it really doesn't matter if depression led to the discouraging thoughts and the physiological is responsible for the condition, or if the discouraging thoughts led to the depression and the soul is the primary culprit. If depression and discouragement are both present, try to alleviate them both. They may have both been present for so long that it is impossible to remember which came first.

Combat the depression with sleep, food, or whatever else is appropriate, and combat the discouragement with reminders of Jesus' love and hope for the future. Neither support will hurt, and in most cases, one is not more important than the other. Both are good, and you do not need to worry about doing the wrong one first.

Once the acute phase is over and the immediate needs have been met, the person is better able to note which is responsible when the struggles resume. Sometimes if you get the discouraging thoughts under control that you think are responsible, you may realize that there are still depressive tendencies that need to be investigated, or vice versa.

Sometimes the most pressing need is obvious. They may be the most selfish person that you have ever met, who also wants to kill themself. Obviously, trying to address selfishness is probably not the way to start. Sometimes, when it is not obvious, just try to help as much as you can with what you can. The path forward can become clearer over time. But the acute phase is not the time to overanalyze; it is the time to start loving and ministering.

At this point you will probably hear a lot of their feelings. Feelings are important. But they are not always true. They cannot be discounted, because they are real and they are influential. They are often the first and most obvious thing encountered. So do not make light of them at this phase, even if they are obviously not true. In my experience, it is usually better to address feelings much later in the process, after truth has been established and the person is confident of it. Then the feelings can be compared to the truth. The feelings do not need to reconcile with the truth; it may be impossible. The person just needs to get to the place where they can make decisions based on the truth, not on feelings.

Feelings are not necessarily indicative of a disorder. Just because you hit your thumb with a hammer does not mean you need to see a doctor. But if other symptoms accompany the event and the pain (It is bent sideways 90 degrees, the bone is sticking out, or a day later you still cannot use it normally), it may warrant professional medical care.

For example, I get very depressed when I work a 48-hour shift on the ambulance. Even when I have a chance to nap between calls, I do not sleep well, knowing that at any second I could get a call and the person's life on the other end could depend on my response time. (This is rare but possible.) By the time I get off, the future is hopeless, my problems are overwhelming, the world is frightening and cruel, and I can't make sense of anything. Honestly, at this point I can't even buy bread. I go to the store, and I feel guilty if I buy anything more than the cheapest bread because there are so many better things to do with money than spend it on overpriced bread. People in much of the world would love to have even that for a meal. Then I feel guilty if I buy the cheapest bread because my health is worth spending on to keep this body serving the Lord for as long as possible. While I am there trying to decide which is more important, I start berating myself for not planning ahead and baking bread, which is more economical than the cheap bread and has fewer preservatives than the expensive one. Then I start criticizing myself for taking so much time to make a decision, because time is also very valuable (especially when you should be using it to sleep). None of this indecision and flagellation is helpful or healthy, and it doesn't happen when I'm not overtired and depressed.

The best thing for me at this point is not to stay up and try to fix my problems. It is generally not to pray; my trigger is not spiritual. It is not to go seek counsel; I wouldn't make sense of it anyway. It is not to dump on my friends, although that seems like it would make me feel better. Staying awake trying to figure out the answers is foolish. Trying to knock out some of the tasks that are bothering me is usually a poor use of time. I know from experience the best thing at that point is just to go to sleep, even if I lie there awake for an hour or two trying. When I wake up, things are not so bad and are much more manageable. I was depressed, but it is not because of a disorder. It is because I forced natural things out of order. This feeling is easily remedied by meeting the immediate need of sleep.

Remember, different things burden different people differently. When Paul was listing all his burdens in II Corinthians 11, he listed a rather interesting one, "the care of all the churches." Now, most of the things in this chapter I can easily agree would be a challenge. Being shipwrecked, beaten, stoned, and so on are easy to see as big challenges. But this is one that most of us would not recognize as being such a large burden. So never take somebody's burden lightly just because you do not understand its gravity.

Minister

When considering how to minister to the immediate needs of someone who is struggling mentally, I would break it down into three steps: alleviating symptoms, managing expectations, and keeping eternity in view.

Alleviate Symptoms

In alleviating symptoms, several areas of the human may be negatively affected and require attention. They are all important as part of the person, although they may hold different weights to different people. Not everybody will be affected in every area. You may need to determine which is most pressing, and it may not be the order I have used in this chapter. Beware of responding to labels the person is using without taking the time to investigate for yourself what the problem is. We have already mentioned Rosenhan's infamous experiment. Take some time, put some effort into connecting and communicating, and determine for yourself which areas need attention, why, and how.

Minister to the body. I start with this point because when somebody is bleeding out, delaying the application of a tourniquet (where appropriate) while sharing the gospel is typically quite foolish. Truly the gospel is most important, but it may be hard to focus on it when you are fighting to stay alive. That can be true in many other situations that we encounter, even if they are less extreme. Yes, God may miraculously fill that starving person's belly while you witness to him or her, but in most cases I recommend starting with the meal first. This is not entirely without biblical precedent, as Jesus often healed people before and sometimes without them ever realizing that he was the Savior. He cared enough to invest in the physical needs of people who never acknowledged him, followed him, or even thanked him.

The first and simplest things you can offer physically to another person are a full belly and a safe place to sleep. Those alone can work wonders at times, and they are very simple and almost never going to cause harm. It is also very challenging to fix

What about grace?

Proverbs 31:6

Give strong drink unto him that is ready to perish, and wine unto those that be of heavy hearts.

Some would argue that because God's grace is sufficient, we do not need medicines or other interventions. This verse directly contradicts that idea. Here the author of this chapter of the Scriptures is stating that wine, one of the earliest forms of medicine, is appropriate for end of life palliative care. He also declares its value as an antidepressant. The Samaritan used wine as an antiseptic. Jesus did not say that they that are sick need God's grace, He said they need a physician. Solomon mentioned the ointment of the apothecary. Several Scriptures mention healing balms. If God were opposed to medical interventions, why would they be portrayed so positively throughout the Bible?

This is not at all to take away from the miraculous healing possible through Christ, the Great Physician and the Balm of Gilead. But Paul, even with that potential present and available to some, never got healing for his thorn in the flesh or his poor eyesight. He instead received grace to endure those afflictions. Some got miraculous healing, Paul got grace. When he wrote Timothy about his stomach ailments and infirmities, he did not tell him that God's grace was sufficient. He recommended medicinal wine. Paul had grace, Timothy needed medicine.

I Timothy 5:23 Drink no longer water, but use a little wine for thy stomach's sake and thine often infirmities.

The truth is that God does not deal with everyone the same way. Some get miraculous healing. Some get grace to live with their afflictions. But there is very much a place when dealing with infirmities of the physiological for medicinal substances, even if some of them may have less than desirable side effects. They are not to be abused, and the Scriptural command for sobriety cannot be ignored. But God gave humans (doctors and other wise counselors) wisdom to know when the benefits of a substance outweigh their potential disadvantages.

problems while you can barely hold your eyes open or your stomach is aching from hunger. If necessary, these are good places to start. Beyond that, good nutrition (as opposed to junk food) has an effect on your brain. Definitely explore options there.

A visit to a medical doctor could definitely be in order. Recently, I was very distraught after a breakup. I thought I was physically unwell as a result. But knowing what I would counsel other people to do, I went to a medical doctor for a checkup. It turned out that most of my symptoms were actually being caused by airborne seasonal allergens, and a couple of antihistamines helped me to feel much better. The medical world can check for thyroid hormone imbalances, scan for brain tumors, and test a host of other things that they have been trained for that could affect your mental health. A doctor may be able to tell you about medications that have depression or anxiety as a side effect. Once again, there is typically very little downside to this basic step. I always recommend it sooner rather than later.

Walking with the person you are trying to love or engaging in some other form of exercise likely will have beneficial effects on the psyche. The benefits here are both short-term and long-term, but repetition and consistency are essential for maximum benefit. Keep in mind that relationships and loving a person tend to go hand in hand, and while some attempts to love and help a person can be one-and-done, many are open-ended in terms of cost, effort, and duration.

Lighting and music can be major factors that affect the mental through the physical. Blue light and bright bluish LEDs can be major depressants. I noticed this firsthand a few years back when I bought some LED string lights for my bedroom and would use them instead of the light switch to save money. I began to realize that when I was tired or depressed, the LED lighting seemed to make it worse. I did some online research and learned that there is a proven correlation between light color and depressive effects. On the other end of the spectrum (no pun intended) are the "happy lights" my friends in Alaska told me about. They help people with depression during winter, when sunlight is scarce, by mimicking its hues. Different genres of music have also been demonstrated to have different effects on people and their mental state.

Since we have discussed how challenging technology can be, putting sensible limits on what can be viewed and for how long, or even taking a complete technology fast could be beneficial. In fact, I would encourage everyone to try a limited tech fast for a month (e.g., only use it for calls, text messages, and emails or something similar). Even friends I know who do not struggle with their mental health have reported much better mental clarity after such undertakings.

Minister to the emotions. This is often the first thing we encounter with hurting people, even before we understand the injury or illness or hear their feelings. Sometimes they are impossible to miss, and other times they are nearly imperceptible. But they can be just as important as the physical, and their importance is not necessarily proportional to their presentation. They are also usually the gateway to trust with a person. Sympathy, empathy, and compassion all, to a degree, involve meeting emotional needs.

Emotions, generally speaking, are purely a symptom. They can be caused by stimulation to the body, soul, or spirit. For example, the emotion of sadness can be caused by the soul affliction of sorrow or by the physiological affliction of depression. Even if this section does nothing to address the root cause, there is much to be gained by addressing the symptoms. If you are on the ambulance with broken bones, do you want to wait until they have set them in the hospital before you are given pain medicine? In many cases treating the symptoms even before the causes can be addressed is the correct order.

A helpful framework is circulating for determining how best to meet those needs. It asks, "Do you want to be heard? Are you looking for help? Or do you need a hug?" Nearly always the emotions want one or more of these three things.

Hearing somebody entails understanding somebody and believing them. Our understanding runs into challenges because we often think we understand someone before we really do. When we rush to our beliefs and understanding instead of taking the time to actually listen to and empathize with the person we are trying to love, it usually results in more hurt and misunderstanding. Unfortunately, there are no shortcuts to loving; it always takes our most valuable commodity: time. A good way to slow down and make sure you really understand every part of the conversation is to reword it and repeat it back to the other person. If you and the other person are not on the same page, you can catch it immediately and keep working through that aspect to try to understand the big picture. Understanding takes time and effort. Even if you are 100% sure you know the big picture from the first sentence, it is always worthwhile to put in the time and make the effort to communicate your understanding.

Believing someone comes with its own challenges. It is especially hard when you know for a fact that the story is impossible. It is fairly challenging when you know it is not likely. Here you run into an ethical gray area. We have conducted many studies on implanted memories over the last 30 years (Nash, 2016). (If you ask some, we've been doing unpublished studies on those long before that.) The BBC published an article in 2016 exploring the ethical considerations of deliberately planting false memories, noting that it had already been done in human studies (Nash, 2016). Whether deliberate or incidental, false memories can be perceived as real by the person with them. But if you do not believe they are real, it is much harder for you to earn trust. This is a book about technology. Would you believe what is exacerbating this false memory problem? AI has been demonstrated to be remarkably efficient at imprinting false memories! The Massachusetts Institute of Technology (2025) has done several studies on the topic. How you deal with the false memories that the other person believes to be true is between you and your conscience. But start thinking about it now, because it is very likely something that you will encounter.

Sometimes, all a person really needs is to vent. They just want a sympathetic listening ear.

Other times, it goes beyond that to wanting help with whatever is causing the emotion. Here you have two extremes. Some want you to do everything and fix the problem for them. Others want to be involved in every step of the planning, and if you suggest something, it is automatically not a good idea because they did not think of it. You have people at every point in between as well.

As an emergency medical technician, I am usually entering situations where I am better trained and equipped to help than most of the people I am trying to serve. As a result, many of my professional encounters look like the first extreme. However, if I still try to interact with people that way at other times in life, it can cause a lot of headaches.

How you approach helping somebody must be tailored to the individual, as there is definitely no one-size-fits-all method here. Some need help clearing their minds and focusing to come up with a solution. Others need help designing one. Still more may need help with implementation. And many will need accountability in the process. The first thing is to figure out what kind of help they want. Then, from there you can discuss if that is the most appropriate way and how to implement it.

In the third type of situation, a person may just need comfort (a literal or symbolic hug). This is frequently true after a profound loss. The person has already vented, and there is nothing left to be helped. But the emotions continue for days or weeks. No advice or assistance can make things better. Comfort is all that is needed. This comfort can be physical, verbal, or even just presence or availability. This can be significantly more time-consuming than the others, because the pain can take weeks or months to heal, and in many cases never completely goes away. These situations can be frustrating because you want to help make things better, and there is absolutely nothing that you can do. You need to make sure the person is worth the effort before you start (they always are), and you need to evaluate how much you have to give. You never know how much availability they will expect from you, so it may be necessary to manage expectations in the early stages. Calling at 3:00 a.m. every morning will likely be harmful to everyone involved in the long run, though it may be necessary temporarily, depending on the person and situation.

In all of these emotional needs, it is helpful to have been in a past situation similar to the one currently presented. If a person needs to vent, you can understand more empathetically and closely. If a person needs a solution, you likely have some things you can share about what worked and what did not. And if a person needs comfort, you know what brought you comfort and can share it more easily. Your bad experiences can prepare you to meet the emotional needs of somebody else going through a similarly rough time.

Minister to the spirit. At times there are spiritual needs. For the lost person it starts with salvation. There is no power of this world that is stronger than the prince of darkness and the evil spirits under his direction. But at salvation, the Holy Spirit from God indwells the believer, seals, guides, comforts, and guards them, and he is stronger than any of the evil and oppressive spirits. God is above all and more powerful than any in this world or otherwise. Once he takes up abode within a believer, the devils cannot get in again, as there is no room for them. Historical attempts at exorcisms are not recommended. Even if they produce a temporary benefit, there is a real danger (according to Matthew 12:43–45) for a lost person, of an even worse fate befalling the recipient upon relapse without the Holy Spirit now residing where the unclean ones used to.

This necessitates that at some point during this process, the topic of salvation must come up. There are a number of pitfalls and misconceptions in society about this topic, and you should be well-versed in your Bible to have a ready answer for them. One of the more common ones is praying a prayer without ever understanding that they are a sinner deserving of the ultimate judgment and punishment: eternal separation from God and all the physical and mental torments that entails. Another common one is believing that a prayer saves them, when the Bible very clearly states that no work we can do saves us and that the mouth's response comes after the heart belief that brings salvation. A third common one is having a knowledge of God but no heart belief and action.

You can find the answers to these and many more challenges in the book of Romans. I highly recommend being skilled in that book for any opportunities that you may have to share Jesus Christ with an unbeliever. It points out very clearly that we are all sinners. Jesus Christ shed his sinless, all-sufficient blood to pay for our sins and took our punishment on the cross. And simple faith and belief on the Lord Jesus Christ is all that is necessary to accept his free gift of salvation. It also addresses the common challenges people face in understanding and accepting that process. It is worth the time to study it.

(As a precaution, please do not lead people to believe that salvation, right living, or true worship will miraculously heal all of their mental challenges. Yes, Jesus could choose to heal their hypothyroidism immediately at the new birth. But, as already mentioned, that is never promised and is extremely rare. Creating a false hope or motive with the gospel can lead to great confusion and mistrust, both toward the individual and toward Christ and his salvation. Just do not do it.)

For a saved person, the challenges related to sin can be dealt with in a moment, but it may take time to recover from the effects. Honesty, humility, and repentance are all that is required to start you on the right path. The Holy Spirit who lives inside the believer will have already done the convicting and made it plain what needs to be addressed. (I have seen

Christians get confused as to why there is a problem with something they "have always done." It is because the Holy Spirit grows us bit by bit and does not overwhelm us by trying to have us learn and change everything at once.) But if there is a refusal to address it, the Holy Spirit can be grieved and other spirits emboldened to harass the believer and potentially even destroy the flesh (1 Corinthians 5:5). With confession, we have opportunity for cleansing. With repentance, we determine that we will not grieve him in that area anymore. Then the testing in that area may take time, but the spiritual battle is won through obedience to the Holy Ghost.

Some people struggle with the concept of God's chastening. They think that every challenge or pain in their lives must be the result of something that made God angry. (Many times these people had earthly fathers or pastors who were a misrepresentation of God in heaven.) I'll admit that, growing up, I sometimes got smacked without knowing what I did wrong. There were even times when I was spanked that I did not deserve it. But every time I have been chastened by the God of all flesh, I have known exactly why it was happening when it happened and that I deserved it.

Part of the Holy Spirit's job is to convict. Conviction is not a game of questions. (Did I do this wrong?" "Could it be because of this?") Conviction is a declaration of guilt. "You are wrong in this area, and this is the punishment!" It is very clear and unmistakable. I believe the same is true for every Christian. (The same is true regarding salvation. The questions "Are you actually saved?" and "Would a Christian really do that?" are not actually conviction. Conviction from the Holy Spirit sounds similar to "You are a sinner separated from God by your sins. You are condemned to eternity separated from God and everything good in a conscious state of torments and misery. Repent, believe the gospel, and allow God to restore you!") I believe conviction from the Holy Spirit is always present with chastening.

Some people, myself included, try to see God's chastening more frequently than it actually exists. I know the many times that I have done wrong. I still sin far more than I care to admit. Then something bad happens. In my mind, I try to connect the two and make the bad thing that happened chastening for the wrong I've done. But the Holy Spirit has adjudicated no such conviction. Trying to make those connections stems from and contributes to an incorrect view of God and his chastening process. It also indicates that we do not understand forgiveness and feel the need for retribution for every wrong done. But it is neither healthy nor beneficial to try to play the role of the Holy Spirit in your own life or in the lives of others. When the Holy Spirit convicts and God chastens, repent and be restored. But do not try to make every bad thing in your life about punishment, or you will live in fear and be miserable.

The challenges related to proximity may not have as good an answer. I know people who try to make an environment inhospitable for evil spirits by reading Scripture aloud or playing godly music. Some also try to ensure there are no items related to witchcraft or idols in their house that would make evil spirits feel welcome nearby. But ultimately, we live in a world where evil is alive and well, and people who attract and even harbor spirits that are opposed to Christ may be nearby regularly. As this is an area where I do not have much exposure, I would recommend prayer, individual studies, and counsel from spiritual leaders such as pastors or bishops to determine a course of action if you believe this may apply to you.

Minister to the soul. This is by far the deepest and most complicated, because it is the very essence of who we are. We are a soul with a body.

At this point, because things are so complicated, I cannot stress enough the importance of ensuring you use the same definitions in your conversation. A catch-all term like "anxiety" could mean the tightness in your chest. It also could mean grief, sorrow, fear for the future, or distress, depending on who is using it and how. Obviously, each of those ideas has a different solution. If you try to apply a solution to the common idea of worrying about the future to somebody who really means grief in the present, you get disappointment and discouragement. And some people's definitions might be a mixture, using a broad, catch-all term to really describe several challenges with one word. So do not get so focused on one solution that you miss other things that may need assistance.

A universal truth is that the soul cannot tolerate the knowledge of good and evil. It is an ever-present burden and curse. Those with little exposure to evil might think they can handle it pretty well on their own. But the vast majority of the population, with their increased exposure to evil in the world today, know that it is overwhelming. The lost in the world have no recourse. The saved have a peace of God that passes understanding. It does not remove or necessarily even lessen the trouble and pain or the responses to it. But it keeps the heart and mind secure from forces that would otherwise crush it. There is also God's sufficient grace for the situation. Once again, this does not change the situation but allows your soul to keep from being overcome even in the darkest, most painful moments.

With regard to imaginations, they must be confronted with truth. When I read Proverbs 18:22, very often an imagination arises (yes, while I am in God's will and presence reading the Scriptures) that God does not favor me. I then stop to thank and praise God for the fact that he does favor me and to think of examples. But if that imagination were not quickly cast down, it would lead to discouragement and possibly depression. When you try to help somebody with imaginations that afflict their soul, determine what the imaginations are and then find the Bible truth that directly confronts those specific imaginations. If the imagination is not true, the Bible will contradict it. If it is true, the Bible will put it into context. Either way, the imagination will be put into its proper perspective and relationship to God and the Scriptures. Confront imaginations with truth.

The biggest enemy to the soul is self. Self-focus distracts from loving God and loving people. Self-pleasure is usually the opposite of doing right. Self-deprecation detracts from the value God assigned to you. Thinking too highly of oneself allows you to walk all over others. Self-satisfaction is like a black hole. The dopamine created demands more in greater amounts, and it becomes an all-consuming, never-ending pursuit of whatever your choice of immediate satisfaction is. The end result of self-focus is often either a self-absorbed individual with no concern for God, others, or right, or a despondent individual who realizes that self is irreparably flawed and impossible to satisfy. When challenges to the soul result in focus on self, the result is never good.

There are several things that we can do to get our minds off self and benefit our souls. Reading the Scriptures, especially the Psalms where we can often sympathize with their author, can help strengthen the soul. So can prayer, singing psalms, hymns, and spiritual songs, praising God, and fellowship with other believers. Focusing on God as sovereign and on

Jesus as our example can help us deal with sorrows and other afflictions. Finding areas to serve others, especially those who cannot do anything for you in return, can sometimes help with the mind.

Manage Expectations

In managing expectations, we need to consider not only what end result we want for the person we love, but also what is possible. We then need to make sure the thinking is appropriate. We all want perfect healing and for the trauma and grief to be gone completely. We wish for the loved one who passed too early to come back. When that is not possible, we wish for the hurt to stop. That is also not possible. We then may wish to go be with the individual we love. That may be possible, but it is not appropriate. At first, an appropriate and reasonable goal may simply be survival. So many times at the beginning of a trial, the challenges are overwhelming. The pain is devastating. The future in the world is bleak. We get to the end of the day and things haven't improved. Then we wonder where God's grace is.

A reasonable expectation for the beginning of the trial is for grace sufficient to get you through the day. When I was taking suicide-prevention classes, we learned a key term: "safe for now." If we could create a plan that made the person "safe for now," that would be a success. If they called again wanting to end their life the next day, that meant that the previous interaction was a success. That class taught me something about managing expectations. We all want a solution that will make everything easier and remove future problems. Sometimes we barely get enough to get us through the day. That is sufficiency in God's grace. Sometimes it seems like it is barely enough to live with, and we thank him for enough to keep us alive in his plan. A little later in the process, it might be getting back to basic life activities despite the pain. Further down the road, we might look to find purpose in life again or to get happiness from the little things. But if the goal is for the pain to go away completely, at some point in life, those expectations must be adjusted.

I still feel sorrow and pain about my grandfather's passing and the circumstances around it. That was over 10 years ago. It will probably be lifelong. Love and grace do not make the pain disappear. The goal is not to get over the pain, but to live appropriately with it. Struggles come in seasons. Some are harder than others. But at this point, I know that trials do eventually become easier to live with. There will not be complete healing of the soul and its memories until the eternal day. Many of the injuries and diseases that affect our mental state cannot completely heal as we crave in this life.

Keep Eternity in View

To keep eternity in view, we must remember that every decision we make now influences our eternal reward and purpose. Do not make decisions in the immediate that will cause you great regret in the eternal. Even if it alleviates all of the immediate symptoms, if it has a negative effect on eternity, it is the wrong decision.

Also, in the immediate challenges, remembering eternal promises can be a source of encouragement. Peace, joy, love, and so many more are available to us. That thought can provide a little strength in the thick of things now.

The goal becomes this: how do we live with them here and now, in the immediate, the best we can, for the glory of God? That can involve alleviation, accommodation, and attention in the right direction. You want to alleviate as much of the pain or other challenges as is appropriate to maximize the potential God gave you in this life. You want to accommodate the areas you know are weak to avoid stumbling or missing out on what otherwise would be beneficial. You want your attention to be in the right place. The problem may never be completely out of sight, but if you focus on it, it seems to grow. Admittedly, at times it may demand your attention. But eventually, it becomes time to focus on and work toward eternal purpose. God has created each of us for a purpose, and keeping that in view helps us to understand how to move forward.

Chapter 11: Loving for the Long Haul

"Charity suffereth long, and is kind." – I Corinthians 13:4a

After the immediate or acute interventions are implemented and having a positive effect, we can start to think more intently about how to live in the long term. This is when we figure out where we are, how we got here, where we want to be, how to get there, and how to avoid coming back here. It will be a collaborative approach between you and the person you are ministering to. It requires much more time and investment than the acute phase, and not everyone will be able to handle it. But take heart, if your role is just to take the injured man to the inn, you have served him well. If you are the innkeeper trying to figure out what to do next, this chapter is for you.

Identify the Triggers

Individual Triggers

At some point, start trying to identify which triggers are affecting the most. Multiple individual triggers could be affecting multiple different parts of the human. Now I do not have enough experience with spiritual issues to be able to say, "This is how you recognize them." I do believe that if you are born again, the Holy Spirit that indwells you will indicate if another spirit is at work in a person or area. But like I said, this is a belief based on limited knowledge and experience. Telling the body and soul apart is easier. If the trigger is related to knowledge, it triggers from the soul: past (memories), present (situations), future (fears), or potential (imaginations). Remember our soul is afflicted and at times grieved or vexed from the knowledge of good and evil. It affects the body, but knowing where it originates helps determine how best to process it. If the trigger has no known cause or is some "feeling," it is likely physiological. "I just feel depressed/sad/scared," for example.

Combination Triggers

Sometimes, both a soul trigger and a physiological trigger produce the same effect. For example, a person may have a known fear that produces anxiety. That same person may have general fear/anxiety that is physiological in origin. Because the knowledge-based fear is easier to recognize, a pitfall awaits. We can become fixated on the knowledge-based fear. When addressing it does not produce the expected results, we become frustrated and discouraged. But the problem is that we overlooked the possibility that there is also a physiological issue. We cannot get complete results by only addressing half of the problem.

Consequential Triggers

Other times a trigger in one part of the human will create a problem in another part that is more important and must be addressed first. But if we do not eventually address the root problem, it will just create another resultant problem in the future. The body can affect the soul and spirit, the spirit can affect the soul and body, and the soul can affect the body and spirit. For example, if a person is dealing with significant sorrow in the soul, it can contribute to depression in the body. Left unchecked, that depression can become a major disorder that needs medical assistance before we can begin to assess the soul. Not meeting the soul's needs can lead to problems that manifest as other physiological disorders. It can also go the opposite way. Anxiety in the body can create fears in the soul. Addressing the fears but not the underlying physiological issue will create more fears in the future.

Take Stock of Expectations

Achievable Expectations

Can our expectations be accomplished in this life? Do we want the "perfect peace" promised in Isaiah 26? I hate to break it to you, but that will not happen in context until the millennial reign. Jesus left us a form of peace. Yet he also said in this world we would have tribulation. The type of peace that we are longing for, that we were created to experience, and that existed in Eden before sin, cannot exist in this world with tribulation. We want pleasures forevermore. But here in time, we experience grief, sorrow, anguish, and many other unpleasant things. Do we want the type of victory where we are never bothered by our infirmities again? As we already saw, some things are going to bother us right up until the knowledge of good and evil is erased from our souls. Our longings are good. In many cases, they are the ultimate form of what we were created to be. But in this sin-cursed world, we may need to learn to be content with lesser manifestations and the hope that we will one day experience exactly what we crave if we are in Christ.

One should not expect to get over “negative” emotions and never experience them again. In this world of good and evil, most emotions, even the disliked ones, serve a purpose. Sadness is disliked by many religious groups today, and if you were to walk into some churches appearing sad, they would think that you aren't right with God. But God used Nehemiah's visible sadness to commence the rebuilding of Jerusalem! This life under the sun is all about seasons, and the happy appearing, joyful season is not forever. Even then, just because a season is majority joyful does not mean that it is pain-free. By the same token, a season can be marked by overbearing pain and still have many reasons for joy and hope.

Recently I was in a more hurtful season of life, yet I still saw God's care for me on many levels. I was distressed that I was still so sad despite God's evident care. People I have been around would imply that because of all the good and care from God, I should be able to refocus and not be overwhelmed by and showing the pain. But God showed me in the process that his care for me was, at times, like a box of chocolates in the hospital. It was evidence that someone loves and cares about me. If hydromorphone hydrochloride does not make the pain go away, that box of chocolates sure will not! It will not make the expression of agony leave my face. But it reminds and shows me, through the grimaces and the tears, that someone is still there who loves me and cares about me. Sometimes it is acceptable to God to display pain on the outside, despite all his love, goodness, and care.

Avoid criticizing in those situations or pointing out his goodness in a way that implies those manifestations should make the pain disappear. No matter how hard you try to focus on the box of chocolates and the person who gifted them, they do not make the pain go away or lessen its effect on your facial expressions. In those situations, trying to focus on the box of chocolates to lessen the pain most often leads to failure. Failure can contribute to an even worse frame of mind. This can be avoided by recognizing that goodness does not make pain go away and that God does not expect us to hide our pain behind a mask of smiling about his goodness. That is a human misapplication of Scriptures.

There were many times on the ambulance when we had a child in obvious pain. Many times they would be sitting on a parent's lap, with that parent hugging, kissing, and consoling them while promising them good things in the future. The child would barely acknowledge it and would continue wailing for the pain. No reasonable parent would expect anything else of that child. I do not believe that the Heavenly Father expects his children to behave much differently. We can be experiencing his touch, comfort, consolation, and promises for the future and still be expressing the effects of severe pain now. This is perfectly natural and does not mean that we are out of his presence or his will.

We may need to slightly change our desires for the outcome. Some people are looking to improve their situation. That is not promised. What is promised in Romans 8:35–39 is that, even in our worst situations, God still loves us. Romans 8:27 tells us that we do not know how to pray for what is actually good for us. The Holy Spirit prays for things we really need as opposed to the things we think we want. Verse 29 tells us that things in this life are given to conform us to the image of Christ, who suffered much and submitted himself to the Father's will even through unpleasant and difficult situations. Sometimes, instead of coveting a better situation, we need to learn to live by faith. Some would have the pain of their minds eased through forgetting or distractions. But as we already saw in Revelation, that is not likely until the knowledge of good and evil has been erased. Pursuing it now can have unwelcome consequences.

Desiring today what is promised in the future is not a new concept. It is, in a manner, what the multitudes did in Jesus' day. They wanted a ruler to come in and fix all of their problems, and they believed that the Scriptures declared that he would.

He will in the future. But first he had to come as a sacrifice. In similar fashion, according to the Bible, we should expect to sacrifice and suffer somewhat in the present with hope of future glory and perfection.

Do we want perfect mental health? The discovery of adult hippocampal neurogenesis notwithstanding, that is not likely to happen. Sure, God can miraculously heal the brain and endocrine systems, just as he can every other part of the body. But those miraculous healings are not expected in most situations.

This is a very controversial area in which many people will take random Scripture verses out of context or make them say things they do not. We have already mentioned the renewing your mind portion and how people try to wrest it by applying an incorrect definition of mind. Another one I hear regularly abused is the idea of a new creature. Simple context for either mention of the phrase immediately shows you that it is not referring to anything in the flesh. In II Corinthians, he contrasts the new creature with the flesh and its knowledge. In Galatians, he is contrasting our being a new creature with the symbolic in flesh picture of circumcision. Also notice all the forms of "be" in II Corinthians 5:17: "If any man be in Christ, he is a new creature: old things are passed away; behold, all things are become new." We are obviously referring to the man who became a living soul again, not the body that was formed of the dust of the ground or exiting the womb again. I do not understand exactly what this entails. I do not understand how I was dead in trespasses and sins but have been quickened. I do not understand how I am crucified with Christ. But context, common verbiage, and common sense all tell me that those verses do not refer to this body. This new creature does not equate to renewed mental health. While it is possible for thought patterns, addictions, mental damage, and the like to be miraculously healed at salvation, I believe that is about as common as miraculous healing from a stroke, cancer, or polio.

Ultimately, when we are born again we do get a new mind in the eternal soul sense. We have new desires, new direction, new determination, and so much more. But this fleshly mind does not get much of a makeover. Consequently, I believe there is nothing improper about using appropriate medications to help this physiological mind perform at its best. This is no different than you would assist any other part of the body with modern medicine, from a headache to a ruptured spleen. We use medications, nutrition, and similar measures to help the body do what the mind wants it to do. Why do we have different expectations for our brains and hormones than the rest of this flesh? Some of the damages done to mental health, both physiological and neural, will be affected as long as we live in the affected bodies. So what is the achievable victory?

Situational Expectations

Different situations have different victories. I will use a couple of examples from my own life to illustrate. I struggle with fear. People who are mere acquaintances would find that hard to believe, because it does no good whatsoever to show it. It definitely motivates me to do my best, for fear of having to live with the consequences if I do anything less. At times, it also has hindered me from taking risks for the Lord or for others. Allow me to share a couple of my struggles with chronic fears.

About the time I was turning 11, I was getting the hepatitis B vaccine series. It was at that point a three-shot series. I was brought up in a culture where crying, especially by a male, was frowned upon. (I was definitely a weeper and not a great fit for that mentality.) For the first shot I did fairly well. It hurt, but I managed to hold back the tears. But for the second shot about a month later, I was tense because I knew how much the first shot had hurt. If you know anything about this, you know that tensing muscles just makes the needle hurt worse. I couldn't hold back the tears. So I had the pain from the needle coupled with the disappointed expectations and the criticism for overreacting. I really do not remember the experience from the third shot. I know I was afraid and did not want to do it, but I was forced to anyway. It seems foolish to be traumatized by something so minor, whether it was the pain or the embarrassment. But from that point on, I was afraid of needles.

I almost passed out one time when I was 17 after they got a needle out for an injection, so they made me sit in a chair to deliver the shot. When I was 18, I got a job at the nursing home, and they needed a titer to prove that I previously had chicken pox and was immune. While I was sitting in the chair, the nurse told me, "You need to breathe!" Apparently, I had not taken a breath since the needle entered my skin, and the nurse was getting nervous.

By the time I was in my late 20s, I was disgusted by the thought of a healthy 160-pound man being afraid of a little needle that wasn't even doing real damage. So I started donating blood. At first, it took every bit of my will to stay sitting in that chair! My heart was racing. Beads of sweat were forming on my forehead. Now, it doesn't even phase me. My heart rate barely increases. The fear response is virtually nonexistent. That is the kind of victory that we all want.

But that is not how it always is. I do not sleep well the nights before my ambulance shifts. The thought of people's lives potentially depending on my partner's and my actions, coupled with the obvious possibility of human error, creates fear. The fear produces anxiety. My heart starts racing, my chest tightens. My soul mind reminds myself that God is in control. He can protect me from human error. And if one does occur, he knows about it and can handle the situation. But that does not cancel the reaction in my body. It takes time for those hormones to rebalance so I can fall asleep. When they are almost back to normal, the process happens again, and again, and again. Sometimes the only way to make my body submit is to take sleep medicine.

It is frustrating because I know that anxiety is having a negative effect on my body and on my ability to sleep so I can do my job well in the morning. I believe that this in my life mirrors Paul's struggles in Romans 7. The spiritual mind is desiring one thing. The flesh is not agreeing. But I do not live in condemnation. Many people read that passage as if the deliverance mentioned at the end of the chapter meant his flesh stopped being a problem or stopped doing things opposed to his mind. I believe they are misreading it. I am living in victory despite the ongoing challenges. This is not because I no longer struggle with those fears, but because they do not control my desires or decisions. (They do still control things like my ability to sleep, and this is extremely frustrating.) I make decisions based on what I know, not on what I feel. Unlike popular teachings, there is no indication that the feelings or responses from the flesh will ever be reconciled to the Spirit's desires.

God created us with different seasons of life, personalities, and ministry paths. It is something that others should not judge us on. Jeremiah is known as the weeping prophet. One of the most striking examples of this in the Scriptures is that of Heman the Ezrahite, who by the standards of his day was an extremely blessed man. Yet he wrote what I believe is the saddest psalm in the whole book of Psalms: Chapter 88. The psalm starts by confirming that he was a saved man, then lists nothing but afflictions to the end of the song. "What are you mourning about, Heman? You have all of these children. You are a leader in Temple worship. You are skilled in music. You have it made!" We do not see what God sees. But God inspired some insight into Heman's life in Psalm 88. We need to support people where God has them, not try to force them to act where we think they should be.

Job was living in victory when he bowed and worshipped (Job 1:20). He was still grieving. He still wanted to die. He was still questioning God. He was still sorrowing and vexed. He was still having sleepless nights. He was struggling with terrors and pains. But despite the questions and difficulties, he never strayed from what he knew. He was living in victory long before he was healed.

What does your victory look like? I just illustrated how the same person (me) could struggle with the same burden (fear) but have two very different-looking victories. What it looks like for you can also vary from struggle to struggle.

Some people seem to think that victory will make them like a monk, separated from all the world's evil influences and always meditating on pure things. But if you are going to minister where the people are, that kind of life is impossible. We cannot remove all of the negative stimuli that might trigger undesirable thoughts or emotions. We can choose to live for Christ despite the influences on us and our flesh. Ultimately, however strongly or feebly you do that, that is victory.

Not everyone will respond the same way or in the same timeline. You can have two people with the same background facing the same struggle, and the acute phase may be 3 times as long for one person as for the other. Do not approach a person and situation with a preconceived idea of how serious it is or how long it will take. Some people may grasp the initial concept and work through it in a week. With others, you may need to explain the same thing 3 weeks in a row before they understand it, and then take the next 2 weeks helping them work through it. (These people grow your patience and are a great opportunity to practice being Christ-like.) Dragging the process out will leave people frustrated, but rushing it will create a crumbling foundation. Be sensitive to individual needs and abilities when considering a timeline.

Live Now for Eternity

This brings us to living for eternity. While love is our primary motivator in this life, eternity is among the reasons further down. While our hope is in Jesus, there is much hope through him directly connected to eternity. Paul stated that our afflictions work a "far more exceeding and eternal weight of glory" (II Corinthians 4:17). That is a small comfort in the present. We also know that our existence here has eternal purpose. It is ultimately to glorify and please God. I find great purpose in pointing others to Christ and his eternal love and gift for them. I also find purpose in prolonging lives on the ambulance so that others may have more opportunities to receive him as Savior or to tell more people about him. Your existence has eternal purpose. It will not be the same as mine. But it is worth surviving and continuing on here in the best possible frame of mind!

Much of the incentive we are taught to look for in this life actually refers in context to eternity. The "good" in Romans 8:28, the "fullness of joy" in Psalm 16:11, the "perfect peace" in Isaiah 26:3, and many others are presented as something we can have in this life; while in context they are presented as something for a future, often everlasting, day. It does appear that we can have little tastes of them in this life. But in the here and now the joy will never have such fullness that it pushes out all sorrow and grief. The peace will never be so perfect that turmoil cannot find a way in.

Trying to say that what these passages are referring to can be achieved now either frustrates us in this life (as we are perpetually short of what they offer) or cheapens the hope they offer to something that we can experience here. I have never experienced fullness of joy. But there is coming a day of eternal restoration for everything that is hurting or lacking. It is a day when sorrow, grief, the deepest rooted traumatic memories, the strongest sensations of pain, and every other negative thing that currently occupies this body and soul will be passed away! The existence we desire, crave, and were created for is promised in the future to those who believe. It will be so wonderful that we cannot even imagine how great it will be with our current limitations!

Avoid False Hope

Avoid giving false hope. If it is believed, it hurts even worse when the realization comes that it is false. If it is not believed, it rings hollow and is evidence that the person making the trite statements has not even put in the effort to verify their validity. I have heard so many cliches in my life that lack any evidence. When a person uses them to try to cheer up someone who is grieving or sorrowful, it becomes depressing or agitating. In short, it just makes things worse. Keep your advice and encouragement grounded in reality and truth. If you do not know something to be a fact, keep it in until you can verify it or determine it to be empty and vain.

Wait on Big Decisions

One of the steps that you will try to impress upon those whom you are trying to help is not to make decisions while in the wrong frame of mind. Despondency drives bad decisions. Bad decisions set snares for the future. So as much as possible, wait until the mindset is correct to talk about future plans. Deal with only what is necessary until the person is in the right frame of mind to begin processing the future and thinking about it rationally.

Use Motivators

God gave us each different motivators to help. What may give you hope or motivation is likely different for the next person. Maybe for you it is love. For the next person it is hope. For the one after that it is purpose. These and more are all precious gifts from God to motivate us to stay the course. So figure out what it is for the one you are ministering to. Encourage them to cling to that and the one who gave it to them during their darkest times. Because he is still alive, hope, purpose, love, and all of the other motivating attributes that flow from him still exist. They are still within reach, no matter our condition or circumstance.

Fix What You Can

Some things are the mental equivalent of a broken leg. They may need to be stabilized. They may need to be set. Or they may need surgery. But the effort to make them right to whatever degree of invasiveness is necessary pays off in the long run. If there is a nutritional deficiency, supplement it. If there is a known hormonal imbalance, attempt to remedy it (under the supervision of a doctor, of course). If there is sleep deprivation, seek a solution. If there are intrusive thoughts, confront them with the truth. If there is a loss causing grief, see if you can salvage it. Do not continue to be a helpless victim of circumstance when solutions are within your reach.

Address the Triggers

Physiological triggers are usually best addressed through physiological means. Some are applied under medical supervision. Others can be implemented by anyone with knowledge and understanding of the principle.

God created order, and wise people study that order, both in the physical creation and in the human body. When those wise people share their studies and solutions, we should use that information and, where appropriate, seek secular help. I am reminded of a story I heard when I was young about an impending flood. The scientists could see the indications of the impending flood, its extreme nature, and catastrophic devastation. Local authorities were sent door-to-door warning people to evacuate. At one house, the gentleman inside stated, "I trust God. He will take care of me." Sure enough, the flood came, and his house was surrounded by water. Some rescuers came by on a speedboat. They tried to encourage him to get in. He responded, "I trust God. He will take care of me." They left, and after a while the waters got so high that he was stranded on the roof of his house. A helicopter flew by, and they dropped him a ladder and told him to climb on. He waved them by, saying, "I trust God. He will take care of me." Well, the predictable happened, and he was standing before God. He got quite confused and asked God, "Why did you not take care of me?" God replied, "I sent the authorities, the speedboat, and the helicopter. Why did you not use what I sent?" When God sends us help and resources, even if we do not like the source, we should strongly consider using them. Not everything needs or will have a miraculous spiritual fix.

Remedy bad nutrition. As we already discussed, there are entire books on how your diet and nutrition stress your body, which in turn affects your mental health. This may be one of the more complicated and time-consuming endeavors, and it probably is not the one I would lead off with. But it is definitely something to consider if you are trying to help someone with a chronic issue.

A couple of obstetrician-gynecologists, Stephanie McClellan and Beth Hamilton (2010), have written a very thorough work for women on that topic simply entitled *So Stressed*. It includes diet, nutrition, and other factors that help the body overcome physiological issues. I was very impressed with it. People devote their entire lives to studying the human body and different ways to improve its state, and then they share some of that wisdom in a book. If you get an appropriate book, you now have information at your fingertips to help people improve their resilience to psychological and mental damage.

Remove and replace bad influences. In many cases negative physiological influences can be removed and replaced with an opposite positive one. For example, staying up too late can be replaced by going to bed early. Country music can be replaced by good classical music. (I hate country music. After my first breakup I found it to be extremely depressing and have despised it ever since. Both the lyrics and the chord progressions are among the sorriest ever written. If you disagree with this opinion, hopefully the rest of the book is still worth it.) Junk food can be replaced with good nutrition. Find the opposite of your challenge and apply it.

Seek help from modern medicine. Various methods are used in modern medicine to improve mental health. We all know about medications. They are simple, fast, and profitable for pharmaceutical companies and insurers. They also come with potential side effects. If you go that route, you need to be aware of the effects medicine is having on you. I had a former coworker who told me her doctor prescribed her medication for attention-deficit/hyperactivity disorder when she was in paramedic school. It helped her with focus at first, but after a couple of months the side effects began to outweigh the benefits. Be especially vigilant if you are giving these medications to children. They often do not even recognize that they are feeling different, especially if they are in puberty and feel different every new day anyway. Younger children may not be able to communicate what they are feeling, but they may express it with abnormal behavior. If you notice changes, definitely discuss them with your doctor.

When kids are starting treatments, there are special considerations. Their communication is not that great. It is harder to know what "normal" should be for them because they all have different lives and growth stages. A parent may notice any negative changes in a child's life caused by medications. But if that child does not have a stable home environment, with an adult who takes enough time and effort to pay attention, nobody really notices if the drugs have an adverse effect on the child. Then they suffer with side effects and potentially begin a downward spiral in their health.

A number of recognized medical interventions are nonpharmaceutical. One of particular interest to me, although I haven't tried it yet, is eye movement desensitization and reprocessing. People who work in high-stress environments with a lot of stimuli can easily become overstimulated in normal environments. When I am in any type of setting with loud noises or moving lights, it is a challenge as my anxiety level very quickly goes to 1,000%. It is not negative stimuli or anything sinful. It is just a physiological response to repeated stressors that gets triggered by some normal occurrences—even certain churches' music! This therapy attempts to retrain the brain not to respond so strongly to those stimuli by stimulating it with lights in a controlled manner. It seems like a very appropriate solution given the nature of what causes anxiety and posttraumatic stress disorder in those situations.

Psychotherapy, also called talk therapy, is becoming increasingly popular for mental health issues. In some cases it has eliminated the need for medications altogether. It is administered by college graduates who have met the licensing requirements in their state. There are different kinds and styles of therapy for different disorders and people. Life coaches or wellness coaches are similar in style, but they are for healthy people and therefore not regulated as strongly. They are not allowed to treat mental disorders or claim to be therapeutic. Despite possible wellness benefits for a person's health, they are usually not covered by insurance. I am hoping that will change soon.

Create positive lifestyle changes. Other practical and lifestyle changes that may benefit mental health include spiritual strengthening to offset physical weaknesses. Exercise has been shown to have positive effects on mental health. Some natural hormone modifiers may stimulate or supplement hormone production. A common example on the markets now is melatonin. Making environmental changes is always a possibility. They can be as simple as turning off the lights or getting blackout curtains if you are having trouble sleeping. Other environmental factors can be so complicated or necessary that they are impossible to change. But it never hurts to review all the possible factors every so often to see if you can improve your environment. Then adding positive influences such as good music, healthy food, opportunities for positive social interaction, and so forth can be quite rewarding on this front.

Soul factors have a lot of help found in the Bible. It may be comfort from God. It may be comfort from other Christians. Praise or worship could help. Trusting in God. Hoping in God. Declaring truth. Beholding God's glory. Repenting of sins. Removing the source of poisons. The Bible was primarily written to a living soul, and it offers far more opportunities for it than I ever could cover here. The key, if you are sure there is a soul difficulty involved, is to follow the Holy Spirit's guidance and discern which tool is right for the situation. You do not use a pipe wrench to hang a picture, and you do not use a hammer to stop a leaky pipe. Absent a miracle, the wrong tool will likely cause more harm than good.

Recall that not every affliction caused by the knowledge of good and evil is inherently bad for you. At times it takes great discernment, coupled with study and prayer, to determine which of the opposite truths applies to a given stressor. Even then, it may not be possible to determine which applies to the life of another whom you may be trying to help. At that point, you have two honest options. You can keep your mouth shut, or you can present both sides of the truth from a well-studied and evenly presented perspective. Then advise the individual to determine which applies through prayer and seeking biblical counsel. Sometimes I may give only the truth that is opposite to what the person needing help is predisposed to, but this can lead people to think I am being contrary or unhelpful. In most cases it is probably best to present both sides. There must be a lot of care and judgment, especially when dealing with these burdens of the soul.

Prevent them. Since soul triggers are often caused by knowledge, limiting exposure to what knowledge you can handle is often a good idea. Many parents do their kids a favor by limiting their access to knowledge in their formative years. As adults, we should exercise greater discretion about what we can and cannot handle and limit our intake of knowledge that could harm us. For example, if the evil in politics gets you down, do not watch 4 hours of political news before bed every night. If crime triggers you, do not read all of the mug shots in the paper. Prevent as many of the soul's afflictions as you can. As the cliche goes, "an ounce of prevention is worth a pound of cure."

Some people's approach to this is to isolate their kids from many sources of knowledge. This approach closely parallels growing plants in a greenhouse. If the plants grow in a greenhouse of limited knowledge their whole life, they stay relatively healthy and happy. But they have no way of knowing what life is like outside the greenhouse. Not only does that create a fertile place for pride, as the plants inside the greenhouse are so much better protected and better looking than those outside, but it also creates a barrier to truly connecting with those outside. If none of them ever get outside their greenhouse, inbreeding will eventually produce stunted, mutated plants. Besides the negative consequences, we desire to reach our neighbors, not just those who live in the same environment as us.

We have already seen that just exposing young people to all the elements of knowledge is harmful. So the solution would appear to be to start them in a controlled greenhouse environment and then transplant them into the harsher elements. The danger there is that in the transition, they can become stunted, shocked, or killed. They do not know how to handle it and then do stupid stuff, not because they have poor values, but because they are ignorant and were never given appropriate knowledge. Many young people start out in the greenhouse, then get thrown out into the real world as adults with catastrophic results. Those who never left the greenhouse can point to them as a cautionary tale of why you should never leave the greenhouse and just pursue a "safe" life in ineffectual ministry. The ones who got out and actually survived point to how ignorant and ineffective the ministry is of those hiding behind the glass. Those who are "stuck" in the greenhouse may feel like it is a prison. The ones who got out and got damaged may resent the lack of preparation that they received for the world. So keeping them in the greenhouse their whole lives has serious downsides and may keep them from reaching the people God intended them to touch. But starting them inside and then transplanting them opens the door for a myriad of problems and strife.

The wise farmers use a process called "hardening off." The young plants are gradually exposed to the elements until they are acclimated, and losses are greatly reduced. Some I know point to college as this time of hardening off. In my opinion, college age is too old. One reason is that you already should be hard enough at that point to go into battle if needed. The other reason is that there is already a huge knowledge difference at that point, and the worldly-wise peers will not be good educators in getting you up to speed. In Luke 2:42–46 we see that Jesus began receiving exposure to outside knowledge about his Father's business at 12 years old. In the following verses we understand that part of what happened from that point forward was that he increased in wisdom, favor with God, and favor with man. The training beginning at 12 helped both his walk with God and his ability to minister to man.

Determine how to handle them. Once we have identified the soul triggers, we need to decide what to do with them. There are four questions we can ask to determine how to handle burdens of the soul.

The first question is, “Is this even necessary?” Harriet Lerner (2004) gave a great illustration of this in her book *Fear and Other Uninvited Guests*. She mentioned 2 years that she worked at summer camps. The 1st year was at a camp for disabled children. Despite huge deficiencies in appearance and abilities, the kids loved and accepted each other and had a great time. The 2nd year was at a regular camp, where minor differences in appearance and ability among the campers caused significant strife and anxiety. Their deficiencies paled in comparison to the handicaps of the first group, who were not burdened by them at all. The burdens the campers had in that second camp were entirely unnecessary. We can agree that they should have been more accepting of each other and their differences. But even if that did not happen, on an individual level they could have accepted themselves and not worried or been burdened by others' thoughts and criticisms. Some things that can burden us are not worth even another second of our time.

Another question we can ask about the burden is, "Can it be cast?" (Psalms 55:22). Some burdens are legitimate, such as the burden of enemies trying to do you real harm. But we know God is ultimately in control. He can bear the weight of burdens that otherwise would crush us. David had much experience with this while he was hiding from Saul. Casting the burden may not ease our feelings about enemies, but it helps to steady our minds and decision-making in spite of them.

A third question to ask about the burden is, "Can someone else help to bear it?" (Galatians 6:2). This verse is in the context of spiritual brethren helping to bear burdens of weaker members in the church. I believe it is also appropriate to ask whether someone who is medically stronger can help us bear the medical burdens. I already have mentioned the possibility that medications and therapy can help us bear these burdens. Medical and therapeutic specialists have good advice. Some have written books that can be a great resource for people who are challenged by their subject matter. People can draw strength from the book's content and share it with others.

Two people can read the same book or the same passage of Scripture and draw very different amounts of strength from it. As a result they have very different abilities to share the load for the kind of burden the passage describes. God has a place for every one of his children in ministry. I do not know where the notion came from that it takes perfect people to serve God. One hundred years ago we realized that he specialized in using the broken. In fact, many believed that God would not use a man until he broke him. So if you are a failure in every avenue in life, but you draw strength, even in your broken state, from God for help, God will use you just like you are to help others who are similarly broken (II Corinthians 1:4). The areas in which we received strength are those in which we are best suited to come alongside and bear the burdens of others. The same principle can be true in the body as well. If a certain diet or program helps you live better in your body, you can pass that on to others much more effectively than someone who was not helped by those techniques.

The fourth question is, "Must it be borne alone?" (Galatians 6:5). Some burdens are ours and ours alone. Nobody else on earth may fully understand them. A good friend, though he cannot understand them and cannot help you bear them, will still stand with you during these times. We may not know the duration. We may not know the reason. Job is a great example of this. I'm sure he wished he could have cast his burden or shared it. But it was his to bear.

Do not forget prayer as an avenue to help with these burdens (II Corinthians 1:11). I do not understand it, and I fear that I frequently underestimate its potential. But Paul said that it helped him, and God is no respecter of persons. So be mindful to pray for those you are trying to minister to.

Then there are the spiritual struggles. Without much firsthand knowledge, this section will be brief.

For those struggling with possession, salvation is the only solution. Exorcisms MAY provide temporary relief, but they will fail to produce lasting results if nothing else takes up that space.

For those struggling with oppression, various things can strengthen the spirit. Prayer, praise, psalms, and so much more can uplift and strengthen our spirits despite the dark times.

For those stressed by the presence, I would advise you to engage in prayerful analysis of what you allow in your life and home. I have heard more than one parent tell of their child who would have horrible nightmares. When they stopped watching shows that portrayed witchcraft on the television or removed objects associated with witchcraft from their homes, the nightmares stopped.

Consider that people may have varying levels of sensitivity to spiritual oppression, and what does not much affect you may seriously affect someone you are trying to minister to. Part of ministry is recognizing that life is not all about us. We must "bear the infirmities of the weak" (Romans 15:1) and make straight paths for our feet so that the lame coming after us can stay in the way (Hebrews 12:13). Be sensitive to not only what affects you, but also what may affect others in this area.

Plan for Healing

Part of fixing things can also entail creating a conducive environment for health and strengthening. If you are creating a space to help these people, pay attention to the environmental details. Lighting was already mentioned. Music or ambient noise can be a factor. Security with things like deadbolts can be helpful. On the flip side, remove things that are weakening. A diabetic should not be in an environment with a lot of sweets. Perhaps going to a flip phone instead of a higher tech one is appropriate. This also applies to the outside activities. Take advantage of sensory-friendly hours at supermarkets.

Try to make sure your church is taking people with mental disabilities into consideration. Unfortunately, these are sometimes places with the least consideration for people with legitimate disabilities and disorders. A church I love has the most obnoxious LED lights in their chandeliers. They produce a strong negative response in people who are sensitive to such things. Another church I visited not long ago had wonderful preaching and an excellent and friendly spirit among the people. But the lights and music during praise time were so intense that I have not been back. Whatever environment you have influence in, whether inside or outside of your home, whether it is a business, a church, or some other organization, try to create one that can accommodate people with disabilities of all sorts, including mental ones.

Your attempts to minister and provide space for people to heal should offer structure. Structure makes so many things in life easier, from nutrition to rest to spiritual endeavors. Setting up a structure to help people is likely to offer a very good return on investment. Accountability systems are also great if they are anchored in love, not in a desire to control or use. These are both very good qualities for your environment to have as you minister to people.

Structure necessitates accountability. Without accountability, it quickly degrades into shambles. Our whole society is built upon levels of responsibility. Individual accountability is a foundational element of the "protestant work ethic" which is stated quite succinctly in the Bible as "If any would not work, neither should he eat" (II Thessalonians 3:10). Accountability for actions, both negative and positive, is necessary for people to function healthily in any socictal structure.

You should seek to provide positive opportunities. Within the long-term structure are four main sources of satisfaction for the individual that may help counteract many symptoms. When God created man, he gave him four tasks: dress the garden, keep the garden, be fruitful and multiply, and steward and rule the earth (Genesis 1:28, 2:15). Incorporating some of these principles in your attempts to minister may help give a more sustainable boost. Your healing environment should include opportunities to live out what they were given to occupy themselves with at creation.

Dress the garden. He was to create, improve, and beautify. Opportunities to engage in art or music can be uplifting. Opportunities to produce, whether something useful around the yard or even a paycheck at work, help bring satisfaction. These, in a sense, fulfill the God-given mandate to dress the garden. God mandates things to us because he knows that they are good for us.

Art and production bring satisfaction. Obviously not every job will, and sometimes you may need to leave a certain job for the sake of your mental health. But being completely unoccupied is hazardous in its own right. I have a friend who retired. Almost immediately he went into what he thought was normal seasonal depression. Six months later he still wasn't coming out. I kept trying to encourage him to get a job for "financial reasons." (There was not much data I could find that says working is good for mental health. But we know men were made to work, and I feel miserable when I am unemployed or underemployed.) In the end, when he finally got a job, his depression symptoms almost immediately went into remission. So long-term help should include encouragement to produce, either art or income.

Keep the garden. He was to maintain the creations and improvements. Things that are produced deteriorate if they are not maintained. Whether maintaining grounds, automobiles, houses, homes, or even making your bed, there is a satisfaction to knowing that you have prevented a decline, at least for that day. Not keeping things not only deprives you of that satisfaction, but it also gets quite discouraging to see things rot, rust, wear out, and otherwise become difficult to use or unusable due to lack of maintenance. A person who has little and maintains or keeps it is usually happier than a person who has much and watches it go to waste. Practicing cleaning and maintenance helps a person's long-term frame of mind.

Be fruitful and multiply. Investing in the next generation brings satisfaction. Whether you are raising a family, passing on skills, or training in the things of God, there is nothing quite like making an impact in people that you expect to outlive you and make things better for those coming after them. You want to hand the baton to someone who will then hand it even further down, making disciples who make disciples.

People who are getting their mental health right may not feel worthy or able to invest in others. Some snobs may not want them around to try investing in them or their loved ones. But that is a step that should be part of any long-term plan to help somebody through their mental health struggles. Start pouring out from what has been poured into you, or it gets stagnant and sours.

One commonly encountered challenge at this point is the fact that people feel unfit or unable to help others. This is because in reality, they are. None of us is able in and of ourselves to accomplish what we aspire to in life. Some of us are just more arrogant than others, continuing to attempt it in our own strength and abilities. God created us to aspire to a purpose so great that we cannot accomplish it without his grace. So that feeling of inability is not a setback. It is the first step in seeking his help to fulfill our life's calling.

Replenish the earth and subdue it. We are to give the earth what it needs to stay fresh and not abuse it. And we are to rule it and order it for our benefit. This takes many forms, from pets to gardens to livestock to grounds maintenance to husbandry to gardening. All these incorporate aspects of replenishing the earth (feeding pets, fertilizing the ground, and so forth) and benefiting from the order we give it. These are longer term commitments that can be quite discouraging and potentially inhumane if handled irresponsibly, so discretion is advised about to whom and when to introduce them.

I had a patient who, in the middle of a meltdown, realized she might be going to a facility and became extremely concerned about her pet turtle. That turtle brought her an outlet to do one of the things she was created to do, and as a result she was very passionate about it and loving toward it.

All of these commands have had cheap technological substitutes. From gardening to reproduction, you can do it in an app. But the substitutes do not produce the same level of satisfaction. In my experience I'm not sure if they have any benefit to mental health. And the same technological pitfalls we mentioned earlier are still present. People may gravitate toward them because it is the best thing they have access to. But for long-term help, you want them to experience these things in reality, not on an app.

Respect Free Will

It is important to remember that, while love wants to fix things for people who are hurting, it also offers a choice. In the garden, God loved Adam and Eve so much that he gave them the most precious thing he could at that time, free will choice to love him back or to gratify their desires in rejecting him. If the relationship is all about control, there is no room to choose and demonstrate love.

So remember as you interact with those you are "ministering" to, if you are controlling to achieve certain results, that is selfish, not love. If you are just striving for an outcome with actions that make you feel better or look good, that is self-serving and superficial. It very likely doesn't help in the long term.

If you are controlling temporarily for their safety, that can be acceptable. Do it as little as possible for as short a time as possible. Take all the knives away if you need to. There are times when people need to be put in paper gowns in a rubber room. Sometimes they even need to be sedated. But these are temporary safety measures, not controlling actions.

Love gives people a choice. Love wants them to choose right. Love may even need to implement consequences for bad decisions. Some people never learn to be responsible and live up to their potential without consequences. Others need mercy. But none need for you to control them, their every action, and the outcome. Offer them grace, the ability to do good. But do not take away their free will in life to achieve the desired outcome.

Seek God's Grace

Recognize that not everything can be fixed. These are the mental equivalent of long-term injuries

Why keep going?

I Corinthians 13:13

And now abideth faith, hope, charity, these three; but the greatest of these is charity.

Unfortunately the prosperity teachings have influenced almost all major religions and destroyed many by providing a false hope. For most, a blessing is not just around the corner. You likely won't see good rise from the ashes of the bad. It is OK to not think positive thoughts or be happy all the times. In reality, the world is sin cursed and degenerating. For most, the situation and burdens will get worse and worse until death. There may be temporary reprieves, but ultimately sin hurts everything it touches. The more sin you are around the more pain and burden you will receive.

If living in a sin cursed world has such a cheery outlook, what could motivate one to continue here? Faith, hope, and charity.

I have faith in an all wise God whose ways are incomprehensibly higher than mine. I do not understand his plan, whether it brings me joy or pain. For my sanity's sake I have given up trying to figure it out. Whatever comes my way, I trust him and avoid trying to rationalize it or predict how it will affect my future.

I have hope, not in anything in this world, but in an "exceeding and eternal weight of glory." The eye of hope looks toward eternity. Everything will be made right. Our relationships will all be perfect with God and each other. We will never know pain or sorrow or any of the effects of evil again. The effects of sin and the pain it caused will never again be remembered or come to mind. The memories that keep us awake at night will be erased, and we will never experience a burden or crisis again! We will experience everything we were created to be without limitations. It will be ultimate satisfaction without any negatives.

So faith keeps me sane, hope keeps me encouraged, and charity keeps me motivated to minster here. If eternity is going to be so great, and it is, the love of Christ shed abroad in my heart wants everybody to be a

Why keep going?

Isaiah 65:17-18a

For, behold, I create new heavens and a new earth: and the former shall not be remembered, nor come into mind. But be ye glad and rejoice for ever in that which I create:

part of it! Every act of service from tying a kid's shoe to writing this book has the goal of reflecting Christ's love to the world. Sacrifice and suffering for the purpose of pointing people to Christ is no less than reasonable when you consider the love Christ has for us and the potential of your witness toward eternity.

This motivation of charity is the exact opposite of most modern psychology and religion. Modern ideology is all about how you feel, what's in it for you, your peace of mind, and so forth. Charity, loving others to the point you put them above yourself, is opposite to our selfish nature, but it is Christ like. As we better understand the great price he paid to leave a sinless glorified environment in heaven, come to earth to suffer the effects of sin on earth, and eventually become sin for us before suffering and dying on Calvary; we become better equipped to live in the sin cursed world ourselves. The whole Bible speaks of the horrors of sin and the potential for a Saviour. Reading it will conform your mind to that of Christ, as opposed to the modern ideology being pushed by the internet, television, peer circles, and other sources.

Isaiah 53:3-4 He is despised and rejected of men; a man of sorrows, and acquainted with grief: and we hid as it were our faces from him; he was despised, and we esteemed him not. Surely he hath borne our griefs, and carried our sorrows: yet we did esteem him stricken, smitten of God, and afflicted.

While we are in this world, our goal is to become more like Christ. At times, God uses sorrow, grief, rejection, and pain to conform us to that image. The end goal is for us to have a deeper relationship with him, be better able to show his love to the world around us, and work his all wise plan both now and in the glorious eternity!

or chronic illnesses. Sometimes things can be somewhat alleviated. Other times, nothing at all helps them. Whether these things are physiological in origin, like dementia, or soul-originated, like sorrow, they cannot be resolved. They are unfortunately the result of living in a sin-cursed world and must be endured until all things are made new.

The final thing is to trust God's grace when you are overwhelmed. The cliche "God will not give you more than you can handle" is hogwash. It makes things better temporarily but provides a nice mess to return to. The truth is that God routinely gives us more than we can handle. For the one who has never met him, it is to point us to him. For one who is running from him, it is to remind us of our need for him. For the one who is walking with him, it is to teach us to rely on him. Psalm 37:23–24 are a great encouragement to me when I stumble in the way because it is overwhelming. "The steps of a good man are ordered by the LORD: and he delighteth in his way. Though he fall, he shall not be utterly cast down: for the LORD upholdeth him with his hand." God's grace helps keep me from falling, and when I do fall, it helps to keep me from being utterly cast down or completely destroyed by the obstacles in my path. His grace is a constant I can rely on through all my difficulties. It is not a miraculous fix. It is miraculous sustenance despite challenges that would otherwise destroy me. He offers it without favoritism to all of his children. It is available as long as it is necessary.

Ministering over the long term is an intense process. It requires a lot of work, a lot of endurance, and a lot of reliance on God’s grace, from everyone involved. The minister and the recipient will both learn and grow a lot in the process.

Chapter 12: Putting Love Into Action

"Then said Jesus unto him, Go, and do thou likewise."
– Luke 10:37

Now that we have all of this information, what do we do with it? The answer is to have mercy on people. The world uses the word "accommodate." The Bible terms are "serve" and "minister," with no expectation of anything in return. Biblically, we should be able to look to our leaders for an example here.

> But it shall not be so among you: but whosoever will be great among you, let him be your minister; And whosoever will be chief among you, let him be your servant: Even as the Son of man came not to be ministered unto, but to minister, and to give his life a ransom for many. (Matthew 20:26–28)

If those examples are derelict, however, that does not leave the Christian with an excuse. We still have examples in Scripture and the Holy Spirit to guide us in each individual situation. To assist in that direction, here is a recap of the foundational principles we learned about sacrificial Samaritan love toward our neighbor.

First, we must notice the need. I hope you are a little bit better equipped to see needs now than you were. But all the knowledge in the world is worthless if you are so self-focused that you do not ever take the time to look around. Look up. See people. We must pay attention to others around us. There is nothing in the world more important than souls.

Then, once we see a need, we must stop what we are doing (unlike the two good law keepers who saw the injured man and chose to keep walking). This means prioritizing other's needs above our own, a core principle in ministry. With this busy, high-paced lifestyle in our world today, we do not ever want to stop for anything. Time is a precious commodity, and we often do not realize that the needs of those around us are worth exchanging for it.

It might cost more than just time, however. We must be willing to spend. The Samaritan gave of his own resources: the oil, wine, and binding. He paid for the innkeeping. The Samaritan gave the innkeeper 2 days' earnings up front for the care of the injured man, with the promise to settle the tab, whatever it should incur. He made a serious, open-ended financial commitment to this man's healing. Sometimes we do not realize how much it will cost us when we start trying to help someone. But they are still worth it. It was also quite inconvenient. The Samaritan put him on his own beast, so guess who was walking the rest of the way to town? Ministering to others sometimes involves spending and using our possessions for others.

Beyond that, it was kind of risky. We must be willing to take risks. Robbers or others may still be lurking around. The man whom he was trying to help could have deteriorated even more or even died on his beast. The ethnic strife in his day meant that he likely would have faced more than disdain or a jail sentence for his “part” in the death. Even today there are risks involved, although not usually that severe. Criticism is virtually guaranteed. If you are trying to minister in any way, there will be people who have problems with the methods you use. If they are of decent character, they will tell you so. If they are scoundrels, they will talk to everyone but you about it. Accusations of hate or other malicious and slanderous charges are always a possibility. You will likely be used by people at some point, and even your personal safety could be at risk. Take risks anyway.

It was likely repulsive. If you have never seen a naked, battered, bloody man lying in mud formed from dust and body fluids on the side of the road, I promise you, you do not want to. Many people with mental challenges today look and talk like they have seen better days. Are you prepared to be seen with people that the religious crowd wants nothing to do with? Can you love and help them despite their presentation?

It took some effort. The Samaritan not only had to perform the physical labor of dressing and moving the injured man, but also had to locate an inn and make arrangements for after he left. All those interventions that were listed in the last couple of chapters are worthless without effort to apply them. At my job, I see many people who deal with stress and anxiety and all their consequences, even panic attacks, simply because of the people they live with. I feel for those people because I know the current economy makes it almost impossible for the average person to move out on their own. Sometimes our compassion for people leads us to go out of our way to minister to them and make arrangements to help them.

All of this requires personal touch and a personal connection. No technology, program, or medication could ever replace this. It is imperative as we minister that we get our hands dirty and actually touch (figuratively speaking, unless otherwise appropriate) those to whom we are ministering. Taking the time and effort to be there with the person will accomplish more than nearly anything else that you can do. Your presence is the beginning and critical component of this ministry.

He did not know if it would make any difference. We minister because of the value of a soul and a love for Christ and our neighbor, not because of expected results. Expectations fuel disappointments, discouragements, and anger. They ruin relationships and become a source of bitterness. The parable ends before we find out if the Samaritan made any difference. The injured man could have died and never known that the Samaritan ever tried to help him. He could have come around and cursed the fact that a Samaritan had helped him. Maybe he would rather have died than been shown mercy by a Samaritan (or Christian). He might have healed and cost less than the two pence the innkeeper was given. He could have been forever grateful to the stranger who stopped to help. The final outcome could have been extremely discouraging, extremely gratifying, or anywhere across the spectrum in between. But the parable ends before we find out what happened, because it is irrelevant. Go and do thou likewise.

> So I returned, and considered all the oppressions that are done under the sun: and behold the tears of such as were oppressed, and they had no comforter; and on the side of their oppressors there was power; but they had no comforter. (Ecclesiastes 4:1)

> Now we exhort you, brethren, warn them that are unruly, comfort the feebleminded, support the weak, be patient toward all men. See that none render evil for evil unto any man; but ever follow that which is good, both among yourselves, and to all men. (I Thessalonians 5:14–15)

If you would like more information about any of the topics covered in this book, pray to God for wisdom and seek wise counsel, either in person or from a book. Be careful not to create an echo chamber by only seeking those who will tell you what you want to hear. Some people are like Absalom. They are professionals at telling people what they want to hear until they get the opportunity to use them at a later time. Also use Holy Ghost discernment, because not every person or every book is telling the truth. If you are truly seeking the Lord and obeying the wisdom he reveals, alarm bells will be going off when you encounter those things.

Finally, as the author who has seen much suffering and pain in the world, I would like to implore you. Prepare for eternity. I wish for you to experience all of the bliss that you were created for, that you long for, that seems almost too good to imagine, when God grants eternal restoration. But if you choose to reject the Lord Jesus Christ and keep doing things your own way, he will allow you an eternity away from his presence. There are only torments, despondency, hopelessness, physical pain, and mental agony there. I wish that everyone who reads this book would accept Christ and have the hope of his future promise of restoration. Once you realize how wonderful it is, you want to share this love and hope with everyone. Go tell all of the suffering and hurting people of the word, "Jesus saves!" "Jesus satisfies!" "Jesus gives grace to get through these difficult days!" "And Jesus will restore you to glory one day!" "Believe on him in faith today!

Annotated Bibliography: Further Reading

As all of our lives and life experiences are shaped by those around us and the materials we consume, it would be impossible to acknowledge all who have had influence on the contents of this book. The following are books that were referenced or quoted at some point. I have read dozens on the topic over the years that I borrowed from local libraries or acquired at yard sales, but these were some of the best. I would recommend any of them for their respective area of expertise. Keep in mind that most do not have Christian authors, so some of their perspectives and ideas will be flawed. Because they deal with real-world problems, some of the issues they reference will likely make some Christians uncomfortable. But they have an enormous amount of helpful information about humans and their mental operations that make these works well worth the read.

Brewer, J. A. (2021). *Unwinding anxiety: New science shows how to break the cycles of worry and fear to heal your mind*. Penguin Random House.

This book is especially useful for asking the right questions about a feeling such as anxiety, then using those questions and answers to either cope with or overcome the feeling altogether.

Edwards, A. (2022). *Full disclosure: Real talk about raw emotions*. Palmetto Publishing.

This book highlights many of the major emotions we may experience and gives biblical resources for how to avoid the pitfalls that they may bring.

Lembke, A. (2021). *Dopamine nation: Finding balance in the age of indulgence*. Penguin Random House.

This book describes some of how society is engineered to increase the amounts of dopamine we create. It discusses the problems that this may cause, such as increased sensitivity to pains and more addictions, as well as presenting nonpharmaceutical methods for dealing with them.

Lerner, H. G. (2004). *Fear and other uninvited guests: Tackling the anxiety, fear, and shame that keep us from optimal living and loving*. HarperCollins.

My favorite thing about this book was how the author systematically litigated a number of things in today's society that commonly cause fear and shame, then demonstrated why that was an unnecessary reaction to things largely beyond our control.

McClellan, S., & Hamilton, B. (2010). *So stressed: The ultimate stress relief plan for women*. Simon and Schuster.

This book has a wealth of great information on how to improve the body's physiological state through diet, nutrition, exercise, and other means.

References

Baer, M., Jr. (Director). (1976). *Ode to Billy Joe* [Film]. Warner Bros. Pictures; Warner Bros. Home Entertainment Group.

Bailey, N. (1721). Mind. In *An universal etymological English dictionary.*

Begg, A. (2002, August 28). Thinking like Christ [Podcast episode]. In *Truth for life.* Truth for Life Audio.

Bierce, A. (1911). *The Devil's dictionary.* The World Publishing Company.

Brewer, J. A. (2021). *Unwinding anxiety: New science shows how to break the cycles of worry and fear to heal your mind.* Penguin.

Brown, T. A. (2002). *Genomes* (2nd ed.). Wiley. https://www.ncbi.nlm.nih.gov/books/NBK21134/

Caruso, C. (2023, January 19*). A new field of neuroscience aims to map connections in the brain.* Harvard Medical School. https://hms.harvard.edu/news/new-field-neuroscience-aims-map-connections-brain

Centers for Disease Control and Prevention. (2023a, February 13). *U.S. teen girls experiencing increased sadness and violence* [News release]. https://www.cdc.gov/media/releases/2023/p0213-yrbs.html

Centers for Disease Control and Prevention. (2023b). *Youth Risk Behavior Survey data summary & trends report: 2011–2021.* U.S. Department of Health and Human Services.

Clement of Alexandria. (1867). *The stromata* (W. Wilson, Trans.). Logos Virtual Library. https://www.logoslibrary.org/clement/stromata/712.html (Original work published ca. 153–217 A.D.)

Colman, A. M. (2015a). Alzheimer's disease. In *Oxford dictionary of psychology* (4th ed.). Oxford University Press.

Colman, A. M. (2015b). Anxiety. In *Oxford dictionary of psychology* (4th ed.). Oxford University Press.

Colman, A. M. (2015c). Attention-deficit/hyperactivity disorder. In *Oxford dictionary of psychology* (4th ed.). Oxford University Press.

Colman, A. M. (2015d). Chronic traumatic encephalopathy. In *Oxford dictionary of psychology* (4th ed.). Oxford University Press.

Colman, A. M. (2015e). Depression. In *Oxford dictionary of psychology* (4th ed.). Oxford University Press.

Colman, A. M. (2015f). Paranoia. In *Oxford dictionary of psychology* (4th ed.). Oxford University Press.

Colman, A. M. (2015g). Post-traumatic stress disorder. In *Oxford dictionary of psychology* (4th ed.). Oxford University Press.

Colman, A. M. (2015h). Psychosis. In *Oxford dictionary of psychology* (4th ed.). Oxford University Press.

DoubleZWWE. (2021). *Brock Lesnar, John Cena, and Chris Benoit segment, April 17, 2003, Smackdown Part 2/2* [Video]. YouTube.

https://youtu.be/wlcEV2yOchY?si=3rltMMR0xV6uI-2a

Edwards, A. (2022) *Full disclosure: Real talk about raw emotions*. Palmetto Publishing.

Everything2. (2003). *Joseph Goebbels.* https://everything2.com/title/Joseph+Goebbels

Forman, M. (1975). *One flew over the cuckoo's nest* [Film]. Joel Productions; United Artists.

Francis, O. J., Kopke, B. J., Affatato, A. J., & Jarski, R. W. (2017). Psychiatric presentations during all 4 phases of the lunar cycle. *Advances in Mind-Body Medicine*, *31*(3), 4–7. https://pubmed.ncbi.nlm.nih.gov/28841578/

Hand, D. (Director). (1942). *Bambi* [Film]. Walt Disney Productions; RKO Radio Pictures.

Johnson, S. (1755). Mind. In *A dictionary of the English language*. Rivington.

Kruger, J., & Dunning, D. (1999). Unskilled and unaware of it: How difficulties in recognizing one's own incompetence lead to inflated self-assessments. *Journal of Personality and Social Psychology*, *77*(6), 1121–1134. https://doi.org/10.1037//0022-3514.77.6.1121

Lembke, A. (2021). *Dopamine nation: Finding balance in the age of indulgence.* Penguin.

Lerner, H. G. (2004). *Fear and other uninvited guests: Tackling the anxiety, fear, and shame that keep us from optimal living and loving.* Harper Collins.

Livingstone, D. (n.d.). *David Livingstone quotes.* Goodreads. https://www.goodreads.com/author/quotes/211925.David_Livingstone

Maslow, A. H. (1943). A theory of human motivation. *Psychological Review*, *50*(4), 370–396. https://doi.org/10.1037/h0054346

Massachusetts Institute of Technology. (2025). *AI-implanted false memories*. MIT Media Lab. https://www.media.mit.edu/projects/ai-false-memories/overview/

McClellan, S., & Hamilton, B. (2010). *So stressed: The ultimate stress relief plan for women.* Simon and Schuster.

Meyers, N. (Director). (1998). *The parent trap* [Film]. Walt Disney Pictures; Buena Vista Pictures Distribution.

Nash, R. (2016, October 5). *Would it be ethical to implant false memories in therapy?* BBC. https://www.bbc.com/future/article/20161003-would-it-be-ethical-to-implant-false-memories-in-therapy

Raffo, D. (1987, October 15). *Mike Tyson and his critics agree his Friday night.* UPI. https://www.upi.com/Archives/1987/10/15/Mike-Tyson-and-his-critics-agree-his-Friday-night/8062561268800/

Spurgeon C. H. (1859). *The sweet uses of adversity.* The Spurgeon Center for Biblical Preaching at Midwestern Seminary. https://www.spurgeon.org/resource-library/sermons/the-sweet-uses-of-adversity/#flipbook/

Spurgeon C. H. (1890). *David's prayer in the cave.* The Spurgeon Center for Biblical Preaching at Midwestern Seminary. https://www.spurgeon.org/resource-library/sermons/davids-prayer-in-the-cave/#flipbook/

Spurgeon C. H. (1906). *A wafer of honey.* The Spurgeon Center for Biblical Preaching at Midwestern Seminary. https://www.spurgeon.org/resource-library/sermons/a-wafer-of-honey/#flipbook/

Stevenson, A., & Lindberg, C. A. (Eds.). (2010). Mind. In *New Oxford American dictionary* (3rd ed.). Oxford University Press.

Stevenson, R. (Director). (1957). *Old Yeller* [Film]. Walt Disney Productions; Buena Vista Film Distribution Company.

Stewart, D. (2018, November 15). *Are Freud and psychoanalysis still relevant?* Alliant International University. https://www.alliant.edu/blog/are-freud-and-psychoanalysis-still-relevant

Substance Abuse and Mental Health Services Administration. (2021). *Results from the 2021 National Survey on Drug Use and Health.* U.S. Department of Health and Human Services. https://www.samhsa.gov/data/sites/default/files/reports/rpt39441/NSDUHDetailedTabs2021/NSDUHDetailedTabs2021/NSDUHDetTabsIntro2021.htm

Tertullian. (1885). *Apology* (S. Thelwall, Trans.). Logos

Virtual Library. https://www.logoslibrary.org/tertullian/apology/39.html (Original work published ca. 160–230 A.D.)

Tozer, A. W. (1955). *The Root of the Righteous.* Christian Publications.

Vijayakumar, L. (2015). Suicide in women. *Indian Journal of Psychiatry, 57*(Suppl 2), S233–S238. https://doi.org/10.4103/0019-5545.161484

Wallace, A. (1998, August 6). 'Ryan' ends vets' years of silence. *Los Angeles Times.* https://www.latimes.com/archives/la-xpm-1998-aug-06-mn-10608-story.html

Washer, P. [@paulwasher]. *People tell me judge not lest ye be judged* [Post]. X. https://x.com/paulwasher/status/1083725482460352513?lang=en

Webster, N. (1995a). Care. In *An American dictionary of the English language* [Facsimile edition]. Foundation of American Christian Education. (Original work published 1828)

Webster, N. (1995b). Fear. In *An American dictionary of the English language* [Facsimile edition]. Foundation of American Christian Education. (Original work published 1828)

Webster, N. (1995c). Grief. In *An American dictionary of the English language* [Facsimile edition]. Foundation of American Christian Education. (Original work published 1828)

Webster, N. (1995d). Sorrow. In *An American dictionary of the English language* [Facsimile edition]. Foundation of American Christian Education. (Original work published 1828)

www.ingramcontent.com/pod-product-compliance
Lightning Source LLC
LaVergne TN
LVHW020718110826
845149LV00012B/2314

* 9 7 9 8 9 9 5 4 5 8 5 0 0 *